Other books from
Annie F. Downs

Speak Love

EXPANDED EDITION

YOUR WORDS CAN CHANGE THE WORLD

ANNIE F. DOWNS

AUTHOR OF *PERFECTLY UNIQUE*

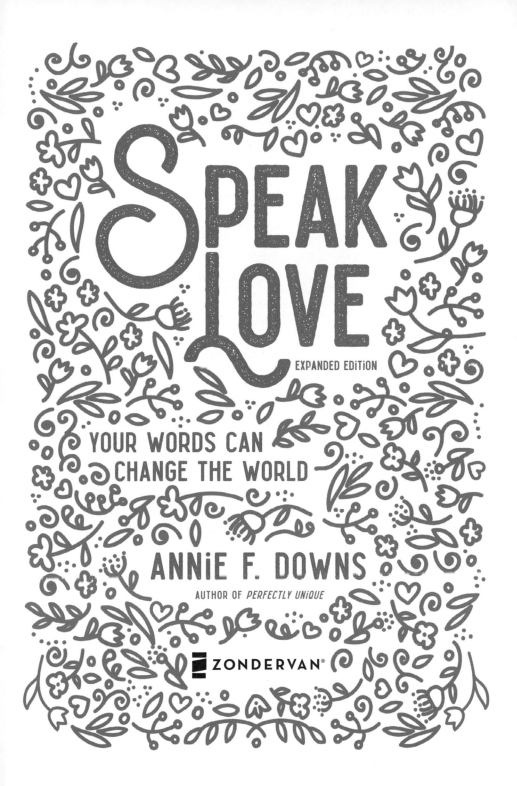

ZONDERVAN®

To Beth Moore.
This is my Gilgal.

Contents

Foreword from Jamie Grace 11

Introduction: Words Matter 13

Part 1: Conversations with God

Chapter 1:   The Power of Words. 23

Chapter 2:   An Apology 33

Chapter 3:   God Speaks Love 45

Chapter 4:   Talk to God 64

Part 2: Conversations with Others

Chapter 5:   Your Family. 88

Chapter 6:   Your People 103

Chapter 7:   The Mean Girl 121

Chapter 8:   Your Online Life 140

Chapter 9:   Celebrities Big and Small 155

Chapter 10: Talking about God 173

Part 3: Last but Not Least? You.

Chapter 11: Believe Truth 193

Chapter 12: Love You 210

Conclusion: Speak Love 227

Appendix 232

Acknowledgments. 239

Jamie Grace

He was "the cute guy" in my circle of my friends. He had "that" hair, the great personality, was a Christian, and could sing and play guitar. What wasn't to like? I remember going to a youth event one afternoon with my sister. There were hundreds of kids there, but I wanted to hang out with "our group," particularly 'cause Mr. Awesome would be there. When we first walked in, I saw him far off with everyone else. They saw me and I immediately headed over. Everyone was laughing and joking, and I figured we were about to have an amazing time.

As I got closer I realized that they weren't welcoming me, and while they were joking it was far from funny. See, they had recently found out about my tic condition, Tourette syndrome, and thought it would be hilarious to mock my twitches when I walked up. I was humiliated and wanted to cry, so I looked over at you-know-who hoping he would notice, bail me out, tell them to quit. He looked at me and blurted out, "Retard!" starting the laughter all over again.

11

I can't begin to tell you how much I wish homeboy had some Annie F. Downs in his life. Yes, this book may be for girls, but let's be real: everyone's going to love it and the whole universe can relate to it. We've all heard someone say something mean, or maybe thought it or said it ourselves, or maybe even been the victim of cruel words. It's a moment where we realize that what we say isn't just random words flying out of our mouths but the chance to either build someone up or completely tear someone down. It may sound cliché, but the words that we choose on a daily basis really do affect others. (And not just people that hear the words! Saying things behind someone's back is also uncool.) And in the long run, the things we say can also change us too. The cool part is, the choice is ours. We can choose to let our words be those that make us feel good for the moment but wreck the heart of someone else, or we can use the words that mirror the kind we could hear our Savior say!

Annie has a challenge for you—for me, for us—to let our words speak hope, truth, joy, peace . . . we gotta speak love.

Jamie Grace

Words Matter

I started writing on February 21, 2006.

Wait. Let me back up.

I've always loved writing and reading. My maternal grandmother was a high school librarian and my paternal grandparents owned a used bookstore, so I probably teethed on novels.

I read voraciously as a child—it was rare that a book was not within reach. I read in the car, when I should have been sleeping, at the dinner table, and in the bathtub. Which, I am sorry to tell you, did lead to a few soaked books, namely *Harriet the Spy* and *Starring Sally J. Freedman As Herself.* Have you ever dropped a book in the bathtub? The panic-induced behavior that follows is hilarious and splashy and full of wrinkled pages and regrets.

I only remember attempting to write one book as a kid, a dramatic retelling of a seventh-grade library book where the main character's best friend is in the hospital. My rendition—written in pencil on lined paper in a three-ring notebook—was three chapters long and absolutely terrible, but the original story was pretty terrible too (and not much longer than my version), so I blame my first literary failure on bad mentorship.

While I may not be one of those authors who wrote books throughout her childhood, I always told stories. Maybe it is because I'm from Georgia and this is the Southern way, but my memories are full of storytelling nights on the front porch or at my grandparents' house across the driveway or down at the local campground every August when it was Camp Meeting. For you guys not from around these parts, quick explanation: The campground is full of cabins and then one big pavilion. Every August, families from East Cobb United Methodist Church go across the street—yes, the campground is literally across the street from the church buildings—and stay there, and they have church meetings every night. And at every meal and in the cool of the evening, people sit around and tell stories. I soaked them up, hearing tales from one hundred years ago in that very spot.

Here's an interesting side note about Camp Meeting: When I was a senior in high school, my youth pastor hit a line drive in the softball game and the softball (which is not even a little bit "soft") hit me right in the nose. And broke it. And I have the lump on my nose to this day to prove it. Check it out next time we're in the same place.

See? I'm a storyteller.

I come from a long line of storytellers and story-enjoyers.

Unfortunately for me, fairly early in my life, ugly crept into the purity of storytelling.

And I started to lie.

My first real memory of lying was in the first grade. Alex, in my class, had a crush on an older girl who rode my bus. I don't recall her name, but she was tall and had stringy blonde hair to her shoulders. I told him she was my cousin. He started bringing toy cars to school to give to her; he would hand them to me expecting me to give them to her since, you know, she was my blood relative and all.

Truth? I never spoke to her once. I lined the cars up on my bookshelf and told Alex that stringy-haired blonde loved them. I told elaborate stories of how she responded when I gave them to her.

Remember, I am a storyteller. It may not have been true, but it was a good story.

It's a complicated tale, recalling to you all the reasons I chose to lie as a kid: to be popular, to be loved, to be right. But I remember thinking that the truth wasn't enough—that it wasn't sad enough, or exciting enough, or dramatic enough. I needed to spice it up. Here's just a little sampling of the things I told people (and these are just the ones I remember; who knows how many more there are): I saw an angel in my bed in sixth grade, I kissed a boy during play practice in eighth grade, I had to go home from a sleepover because I had started my period in fourth grade (when actually I had merely peed in my pants . . . you're welcome for that story), I lost four pounds in one day, and I knew the twin brother of the boy on the *Barney* television show.

Spoiler alert: the actor on *Barney* doesn't have a twin brother.

Here's the kicker: I was a Christian. I accepted Jesus in my heart as a five-year-old, and I meant it. Through elementary and middle school, I honestly was growing in my relationship with the Lord and I did begin to recognize that lying was a sin. I started to feel that twinge of guilt that comes on immediately after you do anything wrong—steal, lie, cheat, whatever. I slowly began to replace the lies with truth, and started spending time reading the

Bible, though sporadically at best. But anytime you can put truth in you, no matter how little, it will wash out some lies.

I grew and matured in my faith, and in my desire to speak truth over lies, throughout high school and college. I knew God had forgiven me and I knew I was actively working on speaking the truth all the time. In the winter of 2006, I was a twenty-five-year-old elementary school teacher living in Marietta, Georgia, and truth was my friend, not lies. I was working through Beth Moore's *Believing God* Bible Study, when she introduced me to a city called Gilgal.

Week eight of that study is titled "Believing God to Get You to Your Gilgal." This city was once the place of the Israelites' greatest defeat. In Joshua 4–5, God brings them back to that place, gives them a huge victory, forgives them, and restores them. Beth says, "Consider our Gilgals the places where we realize that God has rolled away our reproach, proved us victorious in a do-over (an opportunity to go back and get something right), or taken us full circle in a significant way."

That night, February 21, 2006, when I underlined that sentence in the *Believing God* workbook with my green pen, I knew immediately what God was doing with my life. He was giving me a chance to go back and get it right as a storyteller.

So I set the workbook aside and pulled my computer onto my lap and began to type. Six pages later, I exhaled.

Here's part of what I wrote that day, February 21, 2006.

"And here is my Gilgal, or at least one of the parts of my Gilgal. The cycle was one of lies and deception and I believe He's bringing me full circle to a place where instead of declaring lies for my own glory, I will declare truth for His glory."

Those words? That day? That's when this book was born, but I didn't know it yet. I dreamed of being a writer, and now it is my full-time job.

Seven years later, seven being God's number of completion, I'm writing a book on the power of words and how to use your words well to make a difference for Christ.

And that, my friends, is a full circle. Gilgal.

Nice to Meet You

My life is pretty different today than it was in 2006. Now I'm a proud resident of Nashville, Tennessee. I lead a college small group and spend my days writing books, blogs, or tweets, and planning for speaking events. I also hang out with my friends and eat Mexican food every chance I get, go to great concerts and sporting events, and pretty much have a great time. But some of the best moments of my days? Just sitting around and talking with my closest friends.

I hope that's what you feel like we're doing. And now that I've told you that I was a liar as a kid, I kinda feel like we are friends. Just sitting down, across from each other, at my favorite Nashville coffee shop. And with our hands wrapped around warm mugs, let's have a real conversation about God and words and things that matter.[1]

I have been thinking about some things. I've been having conversations with God and other people, and I think we should

---

1   I'll have a soy chai. There are two reasons, which I will now explain: I don't drink dairy and I don't drink coffee. Luckily, I actually prefer the taste of soy in combo with chai tea. (But not the foam they put on top—yuck. That stuff tastes like it came out of the ocean by way of some man's boot.)

talk too. My life in the last year has taken some major shifts and turns—I lived in Nashville, then I was a missionary to college students in Edinburgh, Scotland, and now I'm living back here in Nashville, where I write books and speak to audiences of teenagers. And today, I'm wearing very trendy boots in Portland Brew, my coffee shop/office of choice. And during that transition, I had a realization.

The transition was pretty quick, by the way. Like, some of my clothes still smelled of Scottish detergent kind of fast. One day in July 2012, I flew from Edinburgh to Phoenix, and things have never been the same.

Your Words Matter

I wore my lucky shirt that day in July in the heat of Phoenix. I had only owned it for approximately three weeks, a birthday gift from some of my besties, but I knew it was lucky. Short-sleeved and navy blue with tiny birds all over it, once paired with skinny jeans and sparkly flats I was set to go. It was my first Girls of Grace speaking event and I was ready to rock it.

Or I was ready to throw up. Depending on the minute. Because sister here was nervous. Like whoa nervous.

After leaving Scotland, here I was in Phoenix, Arizona, jet-lagged and scared, speaking on a topic that was new to me: the power of words. Well, it was new to me in the "stand up in front of thousands of girls and talk about it" kind of way. I paced around the church all day while the event was happening, not sure where I was supposed to sit or stand or rest or read. I introduced myself to people who didn't know me (almost everyone), and oh, did I mention this? My table was empty.

Yep, five boxes of my first book, *Perfectly Unique*, never showed up.

So that made me feel like puking too. Not only was I the new girl speaker/author, I was the new girl speaker/author with an empty book table.

(Do you feel like throwing up for me? Thanks. That's real friendship.)

But like the good little soldier I am, I trudged forward. Other speakers killed on that stage all day, and then lunch passed, and before I knew it, I was being miced and it was my turn.

When the host introduced me, she said my book title wrong and was confused by my self-description of being a "nerd." (I am a nerd, by the way. And proudly. DFTBA.[2] I love the library, shows on PBS, sleeping with socks on, the Internet, and playing the French horn.)

So I went out on stage with two strikes against me and an empty book table. Huzzah!

There's this thing that happens when I speak, which is between me and God. It's like the whole time I'm talking I'm totally focused on the words and the audience and the next point, but I have one ear turned upward to hear if God is whispering anything. When I'm onstage, I feel like He is super focused on the moment and we are co-speaking. It's hard to explain but super sweet.

It happened that day in Phoenix. I felt Him with me. And as I talked about the power of words and truth and how we were meant to create life with our words, every sentence became more and more true.

---

2   For the uninitiated, that's "Don't Forget to Be Awesome." Google "Vlogbrothers" and/or "Nerdfighters" now if you haven't before—I'll wait.

Afterward, girls rushed to my table. Yes, the empty one.

Do you know what they wanted?

(Not books, I hope. Sigh . . .)

They wanted to talk.

They wanted to tell me how they were verbally bullied by other girls. They told stories of heartbreaking words others had said to them, how they understood some of the stories I shared. They said to me, "I love Jesus and I want to use my words to honor Him." Moms thanked me, repeatedly, for saying the things they were teaching at home: to use words for good, not evil. Then other women—the youth leaders and small group leaders—teared up and spilled their guts too.

And y'all? I was all, "We've hit a nerve here." I realized the topic was important, but didn't know it was THIS important. I had no idea.

Words. Words have done this.

I was stunned. Insert previously mentioned realization here: Your words matter.

But after many more Girls of Grace events and literally hundreds of conversations with women and thousands of teens hearing this message, this is the truth: Words kill. And words give life.

PART 1

Conversations
with God

When I used to teach elementary school, one of my priorities was learning my students' names. I would stare at each face every morning of that first week and repeat names in my mind until they stuck. Every time I called on someone, I called that kid by name. Repetition was my friend, and within two days I had a good grip on most of the kids, and by the end of the first week, I was money.

I still do the same thing when I meet new friends: I say their name too much. It's probably annoying to some people, but unfortunately for those around me, it doesn't annoy me. So I keep doing it. It ensures that I can remember them in the future.

At least, it usually does. Sometimes, not so much.

In thirty-three years on this planet, I've met a lot of people and I've tried to remember a lot of names. Unfortunately, I think my brain may be full. I keep meeting people and not remembering their names, just like trying to shove just ONE MORE MARSHMALLOW in your mouth during the classic youth group game Chubby Bunny. That last marshmallow usually pops out and takes some others with it . . . or you choke.

I've been choking a lot lately when it comes to remembering names. I accidentally hurt people's feelings and make them feel unimportant, and it makes me feel sick. I am flawed and human, and I offend other humans when I can't remember their names. It's the worst.

But God never forgets. He knows our names, each of us, and more than that He knows our hearts. In fact, He knows how many hairs are on my head and on your head and on my dad's head, though his is a much easier count than most. (Bald joke. Sorry, Dad.)

God knows your voice and loves to hear from you. You don't have to introduce yourself every time you pray, just like you don't have to introduce yourself to your parents every morning at breakfast. He knows you. He wants you to talk to Him. And He is always speaking too. So let's learn how to carry on conversations with God.

CHAPTER 1

The Power of Words

Reckless words pierce like a sword, but the
tongue of the wise brings healing.

—PROVERBS 12:18

God Spoke

Before there was Earth as we know it, there were words. God
spoke long before we ever even took a breath. "And God said,
'Let there be light.'" Genesis 1:3—the third verse in the whole
Bible. That's pretty early for God to start using words. But He
did. God spoke. And the world began. That's it. He spoke and
there was an ocean, and He spoke and beaches blocked the water
from overtaking the land. He spoke and giraffes poked out their
long necks, stars shined, dogs wagged their tails, trees blossomed,
humans breathed.

God could have created any way He wanted to, right? I
mean, He could have coughed out clouds or molded hippos with

His hands; He could have merely thought about mountains and they would be there.

But He chose to use words to create. And it was good.

Every time God speaks in the Bible, things change. You can see it throughout the Old Testament and the New Testament. Whether it is a circumstance, a heart, or a weather pattern, things change when the Father says it or Jesus commands it. Remember? It was THE WORD that became flesh (see John 1:1).

And we are made in His image, modeled after Him. The One who creates life with words, that is our makeup, our DNA.

We do the same thing.

Create

We have two options when we use our words: we can build or we can destroy. The Bible puts it even more seriously than that:

PROVERBS 18:21

The tongue has the power of life and death. (NIV)

Words kill, words give life. (The Message)

And that's true for you too, isn't it? I know it is true for me. I can tell you story after story of how someone's words gave me life, built me up, strengthened me. And I can tell you stories of how words have broken my heart.

They. Are. Powerful.

I know this because I've felt it over and over. But this one time in seventh grade left a defining mark on my heart. Words changed me forever.

That year, my social studies teacher was Mr. Samson. His classroom was the first one on the left. It had lots of windows and the desks were squished together. I sat between two boys and behind my best friend. I watched, one day, as one of the boys borrowed a tiny green piece of paper from my friend Jessica and began to make some sort of list. I don't know how I knew, but I knew that list was about me. I couldn't see it, but watching him write told me everything. I was equal parts worried and curious.

Class ended. Mark ripped the green paper into tiny squares, and as he walked out of the classroom he dropped them in the trash can. After the classroom cleared, I slowly packed up, and with Mr. Samson's eyes following my every move I knelt down and scooped up those tiny squares from the trash and shoved them into the left front pocket of my acid-wash jeans.

(The '90s, y'all. You missed some great jeans.)

I rushed out of the room. I never looked back. I didn't want to acknowledge what my teacher and I both knew: I was going to regret digging in the trash.

I got home that afternoon, and after dinner I went upstairs to my room and spread those squares out across the carpeted floor. Like completing some type of evil puzzle, I mixed and matched pieces until the frayed edges met and the words began to come together. I taped the pieces as they lined up, and since the pieces were so small the paper started to feel laminated with Scotch Tape.

I began to read the text in that classic middle-school dude chicken-scratch handwriting. It was a list of every girl in our class with one word to describe them.

I zeroed in on my own name. And my line looked like this:

Annie = Flabby

It's not even that this was necessarily untrue—I've been overweight a long time. But what hurt my feelings was that of all the words my friend could pick to describe me, THAT was the top one? Seriously? How about "funny" or "kind" or "silly" or "smart"? Those were true too. But "flabby" was the one he wanted to label me. And so it was.

I can still see it. In one instant, I can pull forward that mental image of that piece of paper; probably because I kept that paper until I finished high school. Tucked safely under a box of costume jewelry in the top drawer of my dresser, this ratty green piece of paper survived far longer than any of those middle school friendships or most of the information I learned in that social studies class. (Sorry, Mr. Samson.)

I don't know why I kept it. Maybe it was just to be mean to myself (something we'll talk about later), or maybe I just felt like I had earned it or that it was a prize for my sleuthing. Either way, it broke my heart every time I saw it, whether I pulled it out of the drawer or simply saw a corner peeking out from under the stacks.

In my book *Perfectly Unique*, I tell the story of how I once duct-taped myself in high school to try to fit into an outfit I wanted to wear. Because of the words others had said to me, like in this note—and, honestly, because of the words I had said to myself—I hated me and I acted out of that.

You see, words lead to actions. Words change things.

It was words that wounded me. And words that healed me.

I could keep going. You could too, couldn't you? We could sit here and swap stories until my mug of chai was empty and the coffee shop workers began to sweep the floors and turn off the neon OPEN light. Because if you are a girl, you have experienced the pain of words firsthand.

I know you have.

I know because I've been a girl my whole life. Yes, all thirty-three years of it. And I've known a lot of girls. And I've talked to a lot of girls. And I've been mean to girls.

So. I know you know.

The question is, what do we do with that?

The Plan

We are a new generation. A loud generation. You are communicating all the time. Whether it's talking, or texting, through Facebook or Instagram or other corners of the Internet, you are using your words. So let's chat, for the next few chapters, about how we can use our words to impact our world for the better.

Because, hi, you can.

So here's how we're going to do this:

First of all, let's focus on how you talk to God and about God. Because really, friend, that's what it is all about. Maybe you know Him well or maybe you don't. But my prayer for you, by the end of this book, is that you will see Him more clearly and love Him more deeply and speak differently to Him and about Him. Also, God is always speaking love—are you hearing Him? He is our model, He is our example. How God uses His words is how we can learn to use ours.

As I told you, I've been a Christian since I was five. I remember the day I got saved, and I was serious about it. But throughout my life, I haven't always been good at talking to God. I worried that I was saying too much or not enough. Even harder for me as a teen? Talking about God. The pressure, OH THE PRESSURE, to get my friends SAVED! Everything I said mattered in a life-or-eternal-death way.[1]

It's different now for me. My relationship with God is different, deeper, truer, and talking about Him is like talking about one of my favorite people. Because He is my favorite. I'm learning every day how to speak love because I see how God speaks love to me and to others.

Speaking of people, isn't that who gets the brunt of our words? The people in your world? I think of my two sisters, bless them, dealing with my word struggles for so many years. In anger, I would jab and stab with just the right words to hurt them. On purpose. You see, constructing sentences and finding great words have always been tools in my toolbox. I just used to use them to hurt, not help. To lie instead of tell the truth. To break instead of heal.

(I'm grateful for my sisters' forgiveness. And God's.)

So we're going to spend a chunk of this time together talking about other people: your family, your friends, BOYS, BOYS, BOYS, celebrities, enemies, teachers, those in your real life and your online life. You're using a lot of words these days, sister.

And we're going to talk about *her*. The Mean Girl. She uses her words, doesn't she? I have strong feelings toward her and how we should treat her and, to be honest, I want to get rid of the mean girls of the world.

I think we can do it.

---

1   My poor friends. My poor self. Yipes, that's a hard way to live . . . like someone else's salvation is dependent on YOU. Revelation 7:10 reminds us all to take a deep breath because salvation belongs to our God.

There's another girl who gets our attention as well. You know her. You are her. Believe it or not, the words you use toward yourself are powerful and defining. It would be wrong of me to talk with you about every other person who gets your words and leave off the one who is often the victim . . . you.

I believe in the Bible. It is true. I find hope in it, this massive collection of God-breathed words. And the more we can fill our minds with those words, the deeper our relationship with God goes and the more our words come out of that place. So each chapter of this book is going to have a memory verse. I'm not the boss of you, so I can't make you memorize them. But I hope you will. I really do.

This one has been following me since that first Girls of Grace event in Phoenix. And as I've worked to memorize it I have grown to love it and believe it and breathe it.

PROVERBS 12:18

Reckless words pierce like a sword, but the tongue of the wise brings healing.

Memorize it, my friend. And live it. May the Holy Spirit press on you when you are stabbing someone—or yourself—with a reckless word. And may you see the healing, feel the healing, that comes from the tongue of the wise.

The sun has set outside Portland Brew. I'm about thirty minutes from meeting two of my best friends for dinner at the barbeque place across the street. But this is one of those conversations that I wish could keep going. You know, the kind where you see the clock ticking away but you wish it would stop?

I wish it would stop.

Thanks to the magic of words on a page, our conversation can go on. So let's keep talking and work through how we will change this world by using our words to speak love.

Your Words Matter

At the end of each chapter, you're gonna see this section: Your Words Matter. Because they do. After you read my words, you should use some of your own. This is when I think you should maybe grab your journal, head to a quiet spot, and think through some of what you've read. This section will also give you some verses to read, a reminder of your memory verse, and some things you can do to speak love into your world.[2]

Memorize the Word

Some suggestions: Write this verse in your journal, write it on a note card and stick it in your locker, or use dry erase markers to write it on your bathroom mirror!

> Reckless words pierce like a sword, but the tongue of the wise brings healing.
>
> —PROVERBS 12:18

---

2   And if you want to go even deeper, turn to the *Speak Love Revolution* section at the back of this book, which not only provides devotions from yours truly with lots of journaling space after each, it has even more Speak Love tips and stories.

Read the Word

Here are the verses I talked about, and a few others. I've listed them in the Bible versions I use the most (anything without a translation behind it is from the NIV)—if you use a different version, that's cool. Check out different translations and see what God speaks to your heart!

- Joshua 4–5
- Genesis 1:3
- John 1:1
- Proverbs 18:21
- Zephaniah 3:17
- 2 Corinthians 5:17

Journal Your Words

These are just a few questions and/or thoughts that you can use to jump-start your journaling.

- What part of using my words well do I find the most challenging?
- When can I remember someone being unkind to me with words?
- What does it really mean to me that words have the power of life and death?
- How do I want to be different when I'm done reading this book?

Use Your Words

Each chapter will offer you a little challenge—a way to use your words to speak love. Whether it is talking face to face, writing a note, or communicating online, you'll get practical ways to do what the chapter talked about.

- Tell someone that you are reading *Speak Love* and tell them why. Maybe it's your parents or your small group leader or your soccer coach or your best friend. Just let someone else know why this book and this topic are important to you.

CHAPTER 2

An Apology

When words are many, sin is not absent.

PROVERBS 10:19

You know, I haven't always been great at this, using my words well. And there is this place deep inside that feels slimy and sick and a weird shade of green because there are people who only know the old me—the dishonest me, the word waster, the word blaster—and don't know me now. God has forgiven me and made me new, I know that.

2 CORINTHIANS 5:17

If anyone is in Christ, [she] is a new creation; the old has gone, the new has come!

Thanks to Scripture and who God is, I know things are cool with Him and me when it comes to my past sins. But there are others who have suffered because of my sin, particularly my sin in using words. So before we continue this conversation, I need to apologize.

I had a friend in middle school named Elizabeth. I remember lining up outside of the bathrooms after finishing lunch, and Elizabeth was in line behind me. While we were waiting she asked about my family's trip to the beach over the past summer.

I told her about how I swam out to a sandbar and saw a whale, and that I began to swim alongside said whale.

It never happened. In fact, I hate the ocean. I'm scared of sharks. Like whoa scared.

I'm sorry I lied to you, Elizabeth.

In eighth grade, my friend Amanda and I followed Nancy into our Sunday school classroom one week between church services. We said unkind things. We bullied her. She never came back to our church.

I'm really sorry, Nancy.

At our junior prom, I jokingly called my friend Marie a slut. I never meant it, and she didn't act like one, but it wounded her deeply.

I regret that, Marie. I am really sorry.

My two sisters? Don't even get me started. I could just ball up under my covers and never come out, thinking of the cruel things I've said to them at times. I hope you know how sorry I am, Tatum and Sally. I pray that God has healed the wounds where my words cut you raw.

Shamefully, the list could just go on and on. While there are many stories where I am the victim of unkind words being spewed in my direction, it is also true that I am the criminal.

Even now, as I think about it, my stomach is tied in knots and I cringe at the number of people who have been hurt by my words.

I could shrug my shoulders and say, "Eh, I'm a girl. All girls are mean with their words at times." And that would be true. But I know in my heart, like maybe you know in your heart, that there are people on earth whom I will never see again but were deeply hurt by something I said. Something I may not even remember.

As I dreamed and prayed and thought about this book, I saw all their faces. The faces of friends and family members who I know have suffered because of the things I have said—to their faces, behind their backs, with my mouth or with my typing fingers. And I thought, "I can't write this book. I can't write it because I'm ashamed. I can't write it because I still don't always use my words well. I've never killed anyone—want me to write a book on how not to murder? I can do that and feel good about it. But writing about how not to kill people with words? That's hard for me. Because I've done it."

I'm not perfect. (Gasp. Shock. Disbelief.) And I feel it is only right to look you right in the eye and say that to you.

Proverbs 10:19 says, "When words are many, sin is not absent." In my life, that is truth. (And that's the memory verse for this section, by the way, so memorize that puppy. It'll come in handy, I promise.)

I can picture people from my past whom I have hurt with words picking up this book, rolling their eyes, and saying, "Yeah, right. I knew her when . . ." Or, "Ha, the way she talked to me? The things she said about me? Psssh."

To them I want to say, I know. I knew her then too. And that girl? She can't write this book.

Our Wounds Are Being Healed

As I was deep in the process of creating *Speak Love*, I listened to a session of Passion 2013 taught by a pastor named Louie Giglio. I wrestled so much with this idea—that I had used my words so poorly I couldn't even dare attempt to write a book about using words well—that my spirit was exhausted.

Do you know that feeling? Like shame and forgiveness are playing tug-of-war with your guts? Yeah, that was me.

As I stood in my dining room, outlining the chapters you are about to read, I heard Louie say, "Our witness to the world is that our wounds are being healed by Jesus."

I stopped. I turned around and ran to my dining room table and scribbled that sentence out.

Words have wounded me and words have been the weapon I used to wound others. But Jesus is a healer, and now He's using those wounds to witness to others.

But God forgives, God redeems, God restores, and God makes new.

The old Annie wouldn't have the guts or the freedom to write about the power of words. Words controlled her far more than she controlled them.

The new Annie? Me? I can write this book.

Yes, even though I've been a gossip. And a liar. And a cusser.

Trust me, if there is a wrong way to use your words, I've done and I've mastered it and I've graduated at the top of that class.

Here's what God whispers to me all the time:

You are forgiven.

I made you new.

You are honest now.

Everyone screws up.

You Don't Have to Carry It with You

I wonder if you're feeling any of this too. Maybe you are a senior in high school and you realize you're the mean girl of your class, and as soon as you cracked open this book your skin began to crawl. You could be a thirteen-year-old girl who has picked up cussing this year at school and you feel so dirty about it. Or you sometimes exaggerate the truth to tell a better story. Or you sit back and say nothing when that girl on your volleyball team gets picked on . . . Day. After. Day.

Or maybe you are just a normal girl who can look back ten years or ten minutes and realize that given the choice to speak life or speak death, you spoke death.

I'm just like you.

Here's something you have to quit before you keep reading this book, and I had to quit before I could start writing it:

GUILT.

(You thought I was going to say cussing, didn't you? Or bullying? Ha—I'm full of surprises, y'all. Pure full of 'em.)

You can't bring your guilt with you for another page.

And neither can I.

I say all this to say: While I have received and continue to receive God's forgiveness for the way I use my words, I knew in my heart that I needed to confess to you, and to those who knew me back then, that I am humbled by the topic of this book and my unlikely assignment to write it. I'm grateful that I, of all possible people, am the one to walk this road with you.

Some of Jesus's Best Friends Were Liars

And this road isn't a modern one; people have been moseying down that path forever. That's why I want to tell you about my friend Peter. Well, he's not really my friend, but when I read about him in the Bible, I think that we would have totally been friends.

I get him. He's vocal, passionate, fiercely loyal, a writer, and—get this—he's a bit of a liar. In fact, in the book of John, we read that Peter lied three times, and it was a huge mistake.

Peter was one of Jesus's twelve disciples—like, His very best friends who traveled everywhere with Him for years. And sometimes Jesus would pull aside His three closest guys, and every time that included Peter. So think of your very, very besties, and that is who Peter was to Jesus.

And then, the day Jesus is arrested, Peter does something heartbreaking. Read it.

JOHN 18:15-18 (**THE MESSAGE**):

Simon Peter and another disciple followed Jesus. That other disciple was known to the Chief Priest, and so he went in with Jesus to the Chief Priest's courtyard. Peter had to stay outside. Then the other disciple went out, spoke to the doorkeeper, and got Peter in.

The young woman who was the doorkeeper said to Peter, "Aren't you one of this man's disciples?"

He said, "No, I'm not."

The servants and police had made a fire because of the cold and were huddled there warming themselves. Peter stood with them, trying to get warm.

> **JOHN 18:25–27 (THE MESSAGE):**
>
> Meanwhile, Simon Peter was back at the fire, still trying to get warm. The others there said to him, "Aren't you one of his disciples?"
>
> He denied it, "Not me."
>
> One of the Chief Priest's servants, a relative of the man whose ear Peter had cut off, said, "Didn't I see you in the garden with him?"
>
> Again, Peter denied it. Just then a rooster crowed.

Three times. Just like that. Three times in a row Peter lies, and after years of being one of Jesus's right-hand dudes and saying that he would defend Jesus even if it meant he died (John 13:37–38), he pretends like he doesn't even know who Jesus is. (And to make it even worse, Jesus had predicted what Peter was going to do—and He looked straight into Peter's eyes after he denied Him. See Luke 22:61. Whoa.)

Can you imagine the guilt? The pain that Peter felt between each lie? "I'll never lie again," he probably promised himself, just like you may have done before ("I'll never be mean to her again" or "I'll never cuss again" or "I'll never gossip again"). And then suddenly, much like for Peter, it happened again, and a wave of guilt crashed into your soul and washed you out to Regret Sea.

Peter disappears from the story until days later. (There are blanks like this in the Bible that I wish were filled. I mean, for THREE DAYS the dude is off the grid after lying about Jesus, and then Jesus dies and we don't hear from Peter at all.) And remember that the disciples didn't realize Jesus really was going to rise from the dead. So Peter? Peter is heartbroken. He just lied about his very best friend, and then his friend died, and that's the end of the story. Before he can apologize or take it back, Jesus is gone.

Y'all, that's serious. I can only imagine what he was going through those three days.

John 20 is the first time we see his name again, as he is running toward Jesus's empty tomb. You've got to read John 20, especially if you can relate to the pain of hurting someone you love with words and not knowing if you'll ever be forgiven. What must have been pumping through his guts on that run? I think we can imagine.

I tear up every time I read John 21. Even now, as I'm typing, with my beat-up leather Bible in my lap, tears are just puddling in my eyes. (My blurry vision is making it a little difficult to type, I will confess.) Peter is back to his old job, fishing, and as they are out to sea, they are able to view the shore. A guy yells at them from the sand about where they should be fishing. John sees that it is the resurrected Jesus and tells Peter so. As soon as Peter realizes it is Him, Peter throws on some overclothes and jumps in the water, furiously swimming to the beach.

We don't know all that was said between the two once Peter arrives at the shore, but I bet there were tears. And apologies. And hugs.

At the end of John 21, we do get to listen in on a conversation as Peter and Jesus go on a little walk. Three times Jesus asks Peter, "Do you love Me?"

Three times, Jesus gives Peter the chance to do it over. To do it right. To use his words well. To have a Gilgal full-circle moment.

And then over the next thirty years, Peter becomes a pastor and a writer (including the letters 1 Peter and 2 Peter) and a martyr.

According to the early writers, he died around the same time as Paul (another major dude in the New Testament), which was about thirty years after Jesus was on earth. Many scholars and researchers agree that Peter was crucified. A theologian named Origen wrote that Peter felt himself unworthy to be put to death in the same manner as his Master, and was therefore, at his own request, crucified upside down.

What does that do to your insides? That Peter, this man whose words were his sin, was forgiven, restored, and went on to lead the Christian church in Rome until he was crucified upside down for his faith?

Whoa, right?

Peter was forgiven for his wrongly used words. He accepted that forgiveness and went on to change the world.

We can do the same.

But What About Me?

Do you need forgiveness? Do the words you've said in the past haunt you a bit? You can be forgiven and, like Peter, you can change the world with your words.

For anyone who has asked Jesus into their heart, forgiveness is freely yours![1] The first step is to pray this prayer (or use your own words; this is just a good outline):

God, forgive me for the times when I have used my words to hurt others. I am sorry for the moments when my mouth gets ahead of my heart. I want to honor You with the words that I say. Thank you that Jesus died so that I could be forgiven. Make me more

---

1 Maybe you've never accepted Jesus into your heart and you don't even really get what that's all about. Stick with me. We're gonna talk about that really soon.

like Him. Show me how to use my words to create life and speak love. Thank you for Peter and his example.

Then there are times we also have to reach out to the person we hurt and ask for forgiveness. Have you used words to hurt someone who is still in your life? Pray about it—this may be a good time to make a phone call and ask for forgiveness, or even shoot over an email or text if need be. Sure, it feels awkward and stings and is humbling, but it's a good thing to be forgiven.

And finally there's the hardest part: you have to choose to believe it. Believe that you are forgiven. Because you are! God says in the Bible that when you confess and ask for forgiveness, it is yours.

1 JOHN 1:9

If we confess our sins, he is faithful and just and will forgive us our sins and purify us from all unrighteousness.

Yes, there will be days when you screw up again. And there will be whispers in your ear that there is no way God could ever forgive you for what you've said in the past. But that's a lie. If you confess and ask for forgiveness, you get it. Plain and simple. Choose to believe that truth.

A More Truthful Tomorrow?

So I've got to tell you what I feel now.

Hope.

Lots of hope.

Hope that you will read this book and change your words and your heart before you have a chapter's worth of apologies to make. Hope that you will release that guilt and those old ways. Hope that you can step into the stories of other people and speak the words that will change the winds and bring peace.

I have hope that you can do it better than me. Infinitely better than me.

You have this chance. And so do I. This chance to change everything with words. I know what it is like to use my words to rip a situation to shreds—so I know I can change things. You know that too, don't you?

Now. Let's just do it right, all right? Let's walk away from the guilt and the words made of venom and instead bring healing and joy and peace and love with our words.

PROVERBS 16:24

Pleasant words are a honeycomb, sweet to the soul and healing to the bones.

This isn't a pep talk. This is real life. It isn't hard; it's a choice. In a million different places with a thousand different phrases and as many people as you meet, you can change things with your words.

And I hope you do.

I hope that you will speak love, the way God always does.

Your Words Matter

Memorize the Word

When words are many, sin is not absent, but he who holds his tongue is wise.

—PROVERBS 10:19

Read the Word

- John 18
- John 13:37–38
- John 20–21
- Psalm 19:14
- Proverbs 16:24
- Matthew 5:23–24
- Use your concordance or BibleGateway.com to find out where to read more about Peter.

Journal Your Words

- Do you see yourself in Peter's personality? What parts seem similar?
- Why is it important to ask for forgiveness from others?
- Do you feel shame when you think about how you use your words?
- Write out the prayer for forgiveness in this chapter, or write another prayer in your own words to God.

Use Your Words

- Is there someone you should apologize to for the words you've used toward them? Do it: Write a note. Send an email. Make a call. Get face to face. Ask for forgiveness.
- Thank God for His forgiveness, for how He sees us as clean and holy, and thank Him for His amazing plan for your life.

CHAPTER 3

God Speaks Love

Call to me and I will answer you and tell you
great and unsearchable things you do not know.

—JEREMIAH 33:3

I had always lived in Georgia. For the first twenty-seven years
of my life, I had one state to call home. Though I lived in a
few different cities, I never moved outside of the Peach State
and I never planned to. I liked my Georgia driver's license, my
Georgia sports teams, my Georgia sticker on my car, and my
Georgia home.

Then in October 2007, I felt something stirring in my heart
about Nashville, Tennessee. I was scared. I didn't want to even
think about moving, much less really do it.[1] But I've been a

---

1   I had no friends there, no job, no church, no family. Not even any love for
the Tennessee Volunteers or the Titans, for that matter. Yikes.

Christian a long time, and I have learned to hear God's voice in my life. I knew that quiet voice and that gentle push. I'm not going to bore you with all the details of the story—we'll save that for another book—but fast forward to August 2008, the Sunday I was to move away.

The service at RiverStone Church had just begun. I don't even think the lights were all the way to their contemporary-Christian-worship-service fade yet, and the congregation was singing. I was standing in my usual section, far right about half-way down, and I was alone on my row. Usually our small group sat together; I don't know why they were late. I just remember that no one was standing beside me.

As the music played, tears puddled in my eyes and lots of things ran through my mind: This was my last Sunday at home, everything was about to change, maybe God would change His mind, maybe I was wrong all along . . . Wait. Maybe God would change His mind? "I'm a genius," I thought. "I'll just pray and ask Him to change His mind. He knows I am WILLING to go— I've already paid August rent and I moved one carload of stuff to Nashville. Now He'll let me out of it."

Because, obviously, God is easy to trick like that. (Yeah, right.)

So that's exactly what I prayed. While the rest of the people worshiped God, I bartered with Him. I reminded Him how totally WILLING I was to go. I knew sometimes He doesn't actually make you DO the thing, just be willing to. I begged Him to not make me go. I begged Him to change His mind.

And then, a quietly bold statement ran through my mind and plugged right into my heart.

Nashville is the greatest gift I've ever given you.

I took a deep breath. I knew it was true. It didn't feel true. It didn't look true. But I knew that was God and I knew it was truth.

It didn't feel like a gift for a long time. It felt terrible at first, then okay, then survivable, then good, then great. But I'll tell you what: Five years later? That one sentence that God whispered into my heart is one of the truest things I know.

Nashville is the greatest gift God has ever given me. For sure. No question.

He knew it then. We both know it now.

I disagree with the people who say God doesn't speak to us anymore. I think He is always speaking to us—through the Bible, through nature, through others, through Jesus's life, and directly through the Holy Spirit who lives in us (see Romans 8:9–11).

God has always been speaking. And He has always spoken in the language of love. (I want to make a joke here about "Love in Any Language" because it is an old Sandi Patty song, and I want to tell you the story of how I stood on stage with her when I was in elementary school and did sign language to this song, but that would take too long. So never mind.)

But when God speaks? He speaks love. From creation to the promises for what is to come in the future, God speaks.

God Speaks Creation

As mentioned in the first chapter, when God speaks, He creates. Open your Bible to Genesis 1 and just look at the start of each new paragraph. *And God said. And God said. And God said. Light. Land. Water. Sky. Creatures. Humans.* Phew.

When I taught elementary school, at the end of every afternoon, while the kids were packing their stuff and cleaning up for the day, I would read aloud to them. I loved reading the Chronicles of Narnia, because though I taught in a public school, that book series allowed for me to read an allegorical story about God. It was always my hope that the students would see Jesus in my classroom, so reading about Aslan was a good way to help.

I never read the series as a kid. I was too busy reading things like *Caddie Woodlawn* and the Baby-Sitter's Club series and other fine literature of this type. So I knew very little of the story, especially the story outside of *The Lion, the Witch, and the Wardrobe.*

I was teaching fourth grade the first time I read *The Magician's Nephew*, chronologically the first book in the Narnia series. It was dark outside, kinda stormy, on the day we read about the creation of Narnia. My students were all packed up, book bags were lying around on desks and on the floor, and a few kids were doodling (it was allowed), but most were just listening, leaning forward almost. They had never heard a story like this . . . where there is nothing.

The main characters of the story arrive in a world that is totally dark.

> And really it was uncommonly like Nothing. There were not stars. It was so dark that they couldn't see one another at all and it made no difference whether you kept your eyes shut or opened. Under their feet there was a cool, flat something which might have been earth, and was certainly not grass or wood. The air was cold and dry and there was no wind.

And as the characters stand in this dark, a sound begins . . .

In the darkness something was happening at last. A voice had begun to sing . . . Then two wonders happened at the same moment. One was that the voice was suddenly joined by other voices; more voices than you could possibly count. They were in harmony with it, but far higher up the scale: cold, tingling, silvery voices. The second wonder was that the blackness overhead, all at once, was blazing with stars . . . One moment there had been nothing but darkness; next moment a thousand, thousand points of light leaped out—single stars, constellations, and planets, brighter and bigger than any in our world.

This one Voice sings, and many join in perfect harmony, and then there are stars. As the Voice continues to sing, a sun brilliantly rises and a lion appears. The song changes, and the lion prowls around the world roaring and singing, and grass grows and trees appear. As the lion changes his song, different things are created.

It's one of the most beautiful scenes in literature, if you ask me. (You didn't, but I told you anyway. Sorry.) Every year that I read this book, the creation scene held every kid's attention. It's something you can picture—something you can feel. The power of the lion's roar makes a world appear.

You've got to pop down to the library and check out *The Magician's Nephew*. I'm telling you, just rereading it today has me all in a state of wonder thinking about what it would have been like to see the world created like this. No, it's not exactly as the Bible describes it, but I think C. S. Lewis does an amazing job of giving us a glimpse into what it could have looked like.

It's the sound, the words of the song coming from the mouth of the lion, that made all this beauty appear. Mimicking the creation of the earth in Genesis 1, we see in this story the power of the tongue.

God Speaks Promises

Many times throughout the Bible we see that God used words to make ideas that were meant to last. Creating the heavens and the earth in Genesis 1 is a great example. But I also think of Noah in Genesis 6–9 and how God made him a promise that the earth would never be destroyed by flood again. Throughout the Old Testament, God speaks to His people and makes covenants and promises that stand.

Before He ever told us in Proverbs that words create life or death, He showed us with His own words. The best kind of teacher, I say, is the one who shows you and then tells you.

There's an old saying from my teaching days:

Tell me, I'll forget.

Show me, I'll remember.

Involve me, I'll understand.

If God had merely *told* us in the Bible to use our words well, we would forget it. But He *shows* us so we remember. And because the Holy Spirit lives in us, we are *involved* with Him every time we speak and feel a gentle nudge of what to say and what not to say, and we understand.

We understand that we are made in His image—that just like when God speaks and creates, we speak and create. That's why your voice is so precious.

The Little Mermaid

Maybe you're looking at me—well, what I wrote in the last paragraph at least—and asking, "Um, okay. But my voice doesn't feel all that special. And I'm definitely not generating any rocks and trees with it as proof. How do I know my voice is so precious?" In fact, at a recent Girls of Grace event, one of the questions submitted to our anonymous Q&A session asked, "What if I want to say something but no one is listening?"

Oh, sister. They are listening. Someone is listening, whether or not you are creating stars.

Let's look at this a little differently.

I have a long-standing love for Disney animation. Like many of you, I grew up watching and singing along to the best of the best cartoon musicals in the world. From *Cinderella* to *Beauty and the Beast* and everything in between, those movies are irreplaceable.

Here's what I'm hoping. I'm hoping that when I say, "Look at this stuff, isn't it neat?" that you will immediately want to sing out loud, "Wouldn't you think my collection's complete?" Because you would be able to sing every word of *The Little Mermaid* soundtrack like me.

Yes? No?

"I've got gadgets and gizmos a plenty . . ."

Okay, I'll stop now.

The whole crux of the movie is that Ariel the mermaid trades her voice for the chance to have legs. I know, for you big fans that is a terrible oversimplification of this situation, but it's still true. Ariel's voice? It's her power. It's her gift.

When Ariel decides to trade in her voice to the evil sea hag, Ursula, she begins to sing and this circle lights up in her throat. An evil wisp of smoke reaches into her mouth and pulls out her bright voice. Ursula sucks it into a seashell and cackles with laughter as she realizes that she now has all the power.

She could have taken Ariel's beauty or her ability to swim or her heart or her mind.

But it was her voice. That's where the power was. While Ariel may have gotten what she wanted, she lost her ability to connect and create.

It was her voice.

God Speaks Directly to Us

I think of Ariel as I think about what she lost that day. The entire time she is on land without a voice, she doesn't get to create anything or say the things that are going on in her heart, and it costs her dearly.

Talking to other people gives you a direct connection, and that is what Ariel missed. The same is true when we have conversations with God—both talking and listening. The words are important because the connection is vital. There are many stories in the Bible that we could use as an example of when God speaks to His people and the things He says. But there is one story that stood out to me. Maybe it's because my pastor Pete Wilson taught on it last week and so the story is still fresh in my mind, but when I think about Moses and the burning bush, I realize that God used one conversation to speak a lot of things into Moses's heart.

When you read it, I wonder if you think some of the same things I do—I wonder if you need to hear God speak some of this into your heart.

This story happens in Exodus 3–4.

Moses is just out in a field, and across the way he sees a bush

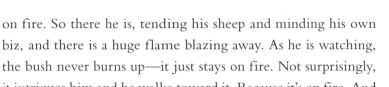

on fire. So there he is, tending his sheep and minding his own biz, and there is a huge flame blazing away. As he is watching, the bush never burns up—it just stays on fire. Not surprisingly, it intrigues him and he walks toward it. Because it's on fire. And not burning up. Yeah, I think I'd go check out that situation as well.

God calls to Moses from within the bush in Exodus 3:4, and for the next two chapters God and Moses talk back and forth. What I see in this conversation is God modeling for us things that we should speak into other people's lives. Remember that not only does He tell us what to do, He shows us and partners with us so that we remember and understand. And live differently. (Grab your Bible, or hop on BibleGateway.com and head to Exodus 3. Follow along as we see how God handles this conversation.)

God is always speaking love. And this story reminds me that He speaks love in many different ways.

1. God speaks love by calling Moses by name.

The very first word God says is Moses's name. I don't know how you feel about your name, but I love my name. And when someone calls me by name, it adds a depth of friendship to the conversation.

2. God speaks love by caring for Moses's safety.

The very next thing God says to Moses, in 3:5, is to not come any closer. For starters, the bush is on fire. (Uh, hey, Moses? Just because the fire isn't burning up the bush doesn't mean that the bush isn't BLAZING HOT. Slow down, bro.) But for seconds, God is there, and because of His holiness Moses can't get too close without God's presence being too much for the human body to handle. So after God calls Moses by name, He immediately says something to show that He cares about Moses.

3. God speaks love by connecting with Moses's life.

God didn't have to introduce Himself, but He takes the time here to remind Moses that He is connected to his whole family line. Have you ever met someone for the first time and they said, "Hey, my name is Harold. I'm a friend of your grandpa's." While you still may not really know Harold, you feel a little more at ease because he's friends with your family. I think God was having that kind of moment with Moses.

4. God speaks love by acknowledging other people's pain.

In chapter 3, verse 7, God tells Moses all the prayers He has heard from the Israelites who are enslaved. When you know that someone else cares about the same stuff you care about, it creates a bond, doesn't it? And in this moment, God is expressing His heart to Moses.

5. God speaks love by sharing His plan to rescue.

I love when my friends have wild plans for adventure and tell me all about it. Anyone you let into your plan is a close, trusted friend. God is showing that He sees Moses as a good friend by telling him what is about to happen. But not only that, He's including Moses in the plan to rescue His people, which I think is awesome.

Then Moses gets insecure—don't we all?—questioning his own ability to be part of the adventure. I want to shake Moses and be like, "DUDE, IF GOD IS STANDING IN FRONT OF YOU AS A BURNING BUSH, I THINK YOU'RE GONNA DO FINE!"

But Moses's insecurity gave God the chance to speak love again.

6. God speaks love by saying He'll always be there.

Isn't that something you want from your friends? To hear them say that they won't abandon you? I love that God said in verse 12, "I will be with you." Just when Moses was confessing that he didn't have the guts to be a part of God's great plan, God reminded him that he wasn't alone in it.

As you continue to read through Exodus chapter three, God lays out more and more plans, and to be honest Moses gets more and more nervous. It's funny; you should read it. God says, "We'll do this!" and Moses says, "But what if they do THIS?" and you just want to punch Moses in the nose for being a doofus.

7. God speaks love by equipping Moses.

As you go through chapter 3 and into chapter 4, God lets Moses practice some things and He instructs Moses and gives him what he needs to be victorious and brave.

And if you keep reading in Exodus—I'm going to ruin the story again like I did for *The Little Mermaid*—you see that Moses leads hundreds of thousands of Israelites out of captivity.

Hundreds of thousands of people, following one dude. Whoa.

I think God built something in Moses that day, something that convinced Moses that God was real, that He was caring, and that He would be beside him. God's words created something in Moses. Where there was nothing—no hope for the people, no courage in Moses—God spoke and it changed everything.

And even now, all the things we are hoping to hear, God says. He said it to Moses, He says it to you.

He knows your name.

ISAIAH 43:1 (**THE MESSAGE**)

Don't be afraid, I've redeemed you. I've called your name. You're mine.

He is your safety.

PSALM 91:4 (**THE MESSAGE**)

His huge outstretched arms protect you—under them you're perfectly safe; his arms fend off all harm.

He is connected to your life.

PSALM 146:10

The Lord reigns forever, your God, O Zion, for all generations.

He knows your pain.

PSALM 22:24 (**THE MESSAGE**)

He has never let you down, never looked the other way when you were being kicked around. He has never wandered off to do his own thing; he has been right there, listening.

He has a plan to rescue you.

JEREMIAH 29:11 (**THE MESSAGE**)

I know what I'm doing. I have it all planned out—plans to take care of you, not abandon you, plans to give you the future you hope for.

He will always be with you.

DEUTERONOMY 31:6 (**THE MESSAGE**)

> Be strong. Take courage. Don't be intimidated. Don't give them a second thought because God, your God, is striding ahead of you. He's right there with you. He won't let you down; he won't leave you.

He is equipping you.

2 PETER 1:3

> His divine power has given us everything we need for life and godliness through our knowledge of him who called us by his own glory and goodness.

And there are many more. So, so many more things that God says to you.

We are so lucky to have a God who cares that much about us, aren't we?

Methinks yes.

The beauty of the New Testament is that at the turn of every page of the Gospels—the books of Matthew, Mark, Luke, and John—you hear Jesus talking. He is God, He is the Word, He is our example.

He tells sickness to leave, and His words create a healthy person.

He tells the storm to be still, and His words create a calm sea.

He tells people they are forgiven, and His words create peace in their hearts.

He tells His disciples that they have power, and His words create confidence in them that didn't exist there before.

He tells the world, "It is finished," and His words create a way for us to be with God forever.

His words? They changed everything. Forever.

And they changed everything for me. For you. For us all.

So How Do I Hear God's Voice?

You want to know how to hear God speak love to you? It's not magic, it's not science, it's just friendship and communication.

First of all, read the Bible. If you want to know what God thinks about something, there is probably a verse in the Bible that talks about it. The more I read the Bible, the more I hear what is important to God and learn who He is.

A few weeks ago, I was worried about my job, being an author and speaker. To be honest with you, sometimes this is a scary profession with lots of responsibilities that make me feel like crawling into my bed and staying there for a year or two.

I was listening to a sermon by Judah Smith, a pastor in Seattle. As he was talking, he mentioned that the Bible says God places us right where He wants us. I sat up taller and thought, "Wait. What? The Bible says that?" So I popped on BibleGateway.com and searched for the phrase Judah said, and came across the verse he was referencing.

1 CORINTHIANS 12:18

God has arranged the parts in the body, every one of them, just as he wanted them to be.

And that was EXACTLY my worry—that I, as part of the body of Christ, was in the wrong place. But God spoke to me through His Word—reassuring me that He has placed me just where He wants me to be.

It changed my heart. Maybe like Moses, I needed God to say that He had plans for me and those plans did not, in fact, include me crawling into bed and staying there for 365-ish days and nights.

You can also hear God's heart through other people—through your pastor, your small group leader, your parents, and even your friends. When you are super sad about a breakup and your best friend reminds you that God is near to the broken-hearted (see Psalm 34:18), that is God speaking love to you.

I also think that God can whisper truths into your heart through the Holy Spirit. Like I told you at the start, there are times when I feel like God has encouraged me and strengthened me, just like He did for Moses (without the fire . . . so far). So how do you know when God is speaking to you?

It's a personal thing, to be honest. Listening to God. And I wouldn't dare claim to be an expert. But just like I know my mom's voice when she calls or when one of my small group girls yells at me from across the church gym, you've learned to recognize the voices of the people you love the most.

So practice listening. You can pray something like this:

God, I want to hear from You. Speak to me. Teach me how to hear You in my heart and in what others say to me.

And then wait. And listen. Journal what you hear. Share it with your small group or your parents or a leader you trust. The best way to grow in your ability to hear God is to practice and let others help you!

Jeremiah 33:3 tells us, "Call to me and I will answer you and tell you great and unsearchable things you do not know." Pray that verse. Like this maybe:

God, Your Word says in Jeremiah that if I call to You, You will answer me. I'm listening.

The Bible is always your best resource when you want to hear from God. There, in black and white (and sometimes red) are God-inspired words for you.

2 TIMOTHY 3:16–17 (**THE MESSAGE**)

Every part of Scripture is God-breathed and useful one way or another—showing us truth, exposing our rebellion, correcting our mistakes, training us to live God's way. Through the Word we are put together and shaped up for the tasks God has for us.

So when you are praying, and you think you hear God whispering to your heart, if what you hear doesn't match up with the Bible, it isn't true. Example? If you hear, "God thinks you are ugly"—no way. Not true. The Bible says that God made you on purpose and that He thinks you are beautiful. Just read Psalm 139.

There are lots of great resources on how to hear the voice of God. One of my favorite books is *Discerning the Voice of God: How to Recognize When God is Speaking* by Priscilla Shirer.

The point? The point is that GOD SPEAKS LOVE. You can see it in your life, you can see it in the Bible, you can see it in nature that He created with a word. God said. And there was light. And there was love.

You are one tough cookie. This chapter has not been easy to navigate, I know. It's intense. But here's the thing I want you to know right now: This isn't a defensive, sit-back kind of book. That's not the kind of women we want to be—sit-back kind of women. There is power in your tongue, and there isn't going to be a page where I let you forget that. This is an offensive book—not offensive like I hope you are offended (I hope you aren't offended), but offensive like a battle plan. If you dive into this, and look for God in these pages and in your life, if you change how you are currently using your words, here's what I promise: your life will be different. Your friendships will be different. Your family will be different.

Dare I say the world will be different?

I dare.

The world could change because of your words. It changed because of God's words, and it changed because of Jesus's words. And that's the model by which you were formed.

You are made in God's image. So all these words and all these verses and all these thoughts in these last few pages have one goal: to help us remember that our words have power because God's words have power.

Let's learn how to use them well.

Your Words Matter

Memorize the Word

> Call to me and I will answer you and tell you great and unsearchable things you do not know.
>
> —JEREMIAH 33:3

Read the Word

There are LOTS of verses used in this chapter, because the Bible is the best resource for learning how God speaks to us. Here are a few of them again:

- Romans 8:9–11
- Genesis 6–9
- Exodus 3–4
- Psalm 146:10
- Deuteronomy 31:6
- Isaiah 43:1
- Psalm 91:4
- Psalm 22:24
- Psalm 139
- Jeremiah 29:11
- 2 Peter 1:3
- Psalm 34:18
- 1 Corinthians 12:18
- 2 Timothy 3:16–17
- Use your concordance or BibleGateway.com to search about other places where the term "God said" or "God speaks" is used.
- Check out more of what Jesus says throughout Matthew, Mark, Luke, and John. Some Bibles even have Jesus's words written in red, which makes it super easy to hear from Him.

Journal Your Words

- Write out your favorite verse from this chapter. Why did that one stick out to you?

- What does it look like to practice hearing the voice of God?
- What ways do you see that you were made in God's image?
- Do you think you are like Moses? How?

Use Your Words

This chapter is more about listening than speaking. So take some time, grab your journal and your Bible, and head to a quiet place. Maybe that's your bedroom, or the big rock down by the lake, or your backyard. Journal and pray and listen to God. Ask Him, "God, what do You think about me?" and listen for truth. Write it down. Believe it.

CHAPTER 4

Talk to God

> I will sing of your strength, in the morning I will
> sing of your love; for you are my fortress, my
> refuge in times of trouble.
>
> —PSALM 59:16

I clearly remember the first time God answered my prayers.

Indulge me, if you don't mind, as I tell you a story from when I was in the third grade. I mentioned it in *Perfectly Unique*, but I can retell it with ease because it is one of the strongest memories I have about my faith as a child.

No, not about how my third-grade boyfriend quoted *Cinderella* to woo me. In the lunch line.

No, not how I wore one of my dad's T-shirts with a belt and thought everyone else would think it was a cool dress.

No, not how I cried when the boy in the desk next to me looked up a bad word in the dictionary and leaned across the desks to show me. It scared me, so I cried. (Wee bit sheltered, I was.)

In the spring of my third-grade year, I starred in our church's children's musical. Okay, to say I was "THE STAR" is a bit of an exaggeration because, while it was true in my heart, I'm pretty sure I was just one of the stars. Fine, one of the cast members.

I was Little Psalty. (For those who don't remember, or have never known, Psalty is a singing hymnal who teaches children about God.) I strapped on this huge blue cardboard costume shaped like a hymnal and threw a baseball bat over my shoulder. I then was to walk through the crowd singing "Take My Life and Let It Be," a beautiful old hymn written by Fanny Crosby.

Oh, did I mention I was a male character? So that's a special part of the story. Hi, my name is Annie, and the only time I got an almost-starring role in a live performance, I end up playing a little boy hymnal.

It was the biggest theatrical performance of the first nine years of my life. And to be honest, it was probably the biggest theatrical performance of the first thirty-three years of my life.

When I got home from school the day of the musical, my mom was in her bed, all the lights off in her room. She had a migraine.

My life is full of memories of migraines. When I was a kid we took my mother to the hospital for them or left the house with my dad so she would have peace and quiet, so I knew immediately that it was bad.

(And in the last fifteen years or so migraines have become an unfortunate part of my adult life as well.)

She whispered to me in her headache voice that she was

sorry, but she wasn't going to be able to make it to the performance that night.

Well, my tender little third-grade heart was broken.

I ran up the stairs to my room, threw my book bag on the floor, knelt down beside my bed, clasped my hands together, and prayed as hard as my heart knew how to pray.

I don't recall every word spoken during that fervent kid prayer; I know I prayed God would heal Mama's headache so she could come to the performance. I begged like only a nine-year-old knows how, with eyes squeezed tight and repeating the same few phrases over and over again.

While I don't remember the words, I remember the feeling. The urgency. The worry. The panic. The desperation.

Mom was still in bed when I left, and I was crushed by the fact she wasn't coming. Even as a child I was a bit dramatic, so when I think about that night I think about a gray cloud floating above my head.

With just minutes until the curtain went up (yes, our church gym had a stage with a legit curtain. I was a privileged child), someone whispered my name. I was standing on the risers, ready to sing, and there was my mom, on the side of the stage, telling me she had made it!

I know. It's like a Hallmark Movie moment.

God answered my prayers. Mom was unable to get out of bed when I left for the performance, and there she was, standing stage left.

I talked to Him, He heard me, and He answered in such a way that I will always have a memory of His ability to heal.

And that's when I learned, for the first time, that prayer is powerful.

JAMES 5:16

Confess your sins to each other and pray for each other so that you may be healed. The prayer of a righteous [person] is powerful and effective.

People get healed. Things change on earth and in the spiritual realm. I mean, if we had all the pages in the world, I would recount for you all the stories in the Bible where someone prayed and God moved. Because, my friend, there are a lot.

God Is Listening

Prayer isn't magical exactly; that's not the right word. But it is otherworldly. It is this amazing opportunity to connect directly with the greatest Being who has always been. Not only are you getting to talk to Him, but He is talking to you.

Wrap your mind around that and then call and tell me how you did it.

But for some reason, even knowing how well we are known by Him, talking to God can be so easy and so difficult at the same time.

(You're welcome for such an insightful statement.)

Here's why: talking to God is super easy because He is everywhere and He is listening. But talking to God can feel super hard because, well, He's invisible.

But your ability to see Him does not determine His ability to exist. He's absolutely real. And He is listening.

Like with every other friend you have, there is an element of talking and listening needed to make for real conversation and to grow your relationship with God. And no matter what someone has said to you, or what you hear in your head, you are never too young to enter into important and life-changing conversations with God.

1 TIMOTHY 4:12

Don't let anyone look down on you because you are young, but set an example for the believers in speech, in life, in love, in faith and in purity.

We've talked about listening to God and what it is like to allow Him to speak love to us. When the world feels like it is too much or too evil or too hard, His love is the whisper in my heart that reminds me not to quit. I'm praying today that you are feeling that—the understanding, deep in your knower, that you aren't too young to hear from God, you aren't too messed up to know His love, and you aren't too busy to speak love to Him.

Some things that we need to remember when it comes to talking to God:

1. He is holy.

You know, it's only because of the sacrifice Jesus made that we can even speak straight to God. Before Jesus? The priests talked to God on behalf of the people. Now the veil has been torn (see Matthew 27:50–54) and we have access straight to God. He is perfect and holy while we are sinful. But Jesus covers our sins, we are clean, and God sees us that way. I think I take that for granted—the fact that God is always accessible now. But He is. He is right there, waiting for you to speak to Him about all the things that matter to you. But remember when you talk to Him, He is a King. He is THE King. Be respectful.

2. He can handle your crazy.

Sometimes I worry, "I can't say that to God." Because maybe I think it is stupid, or the "wrong" thing to pray, or that He doesn't want to hear. Or worse? Sometimes I think I can't express anger or sadness to God. But if my feelings are hurt because something didn't work out the way I wanted it to, I don't have to pretend with God. He can handle my crazy. Here's the truth—He can handle yours too. He's very big. What you're going to say won't shock His solar system. While He is holy and worthy of your respect (see #1), He can handle your honesty too.

3. He is loving.

Meanwhile, while God is handling our crazy, He's also loving us so much. It's really nice of Him. I think it is important to remember, when you are talking to God, that He is all-loving. You don't always get what you want when you pray, but it doesn't mean you should stop praying or that God doesn't love you. Keep praying. Keep worshiping. Keep believing. (Don't stop believin'? Journey song? You're welcome.) When you love someone, you love talking to them, being around them, listening to their dreams and hopes and worries. This is how God feels about you. Always.

4. He is always listening.

There's not a time when you're going to cry out to Him and He's going to ignore you, or be sleeping, or be busy tending to someone else's crazy. Part of the mystery of God is His omnipresence, His ability to be everywhere. He always has time for you, He is always available. So whether it is first thing when you wake up, in the middle of the night, or in the middle of science class, you can talk to Him. He is listening.

5. He is worthy.

One major way we talk to God is through worship and praise. We'll get there in a minute, but a key thing we need to remember is that God deserves our worship. No matter what your circumstances are, no matter if things are good or bad or both (as they usually are), He is worthy. He is always good, always loving, and the One who created everything. Things may not go the way you want them to, but He is still worthy.

Let's Get Personal

If you've spent more than thirty minutes in a Sunday school class or youth group, this chapter might feel commonplace. You've heard this stuff—about praying and reading your Bible and all that jazz, but I'm hoping you'll read with an open mind and open heart.

I grew up in youth group too. From age ten to eighteen-ish, if the church doors were open and the Coke machine was taking quarters, I was there. I heard the same talk, the same topics covered for years and years. I know it can seem redundant. But there is nothing boring about a God who is alive and cares about us. Other religions worship gods who are long dead. But the hope we have? The truth we have? Our God is alive. And how we speak love to God, and how He speaks love to us, affects every area of our lives.

I think there are a few ways we can all talk to God on a daily basis. You don't have to do them all for two hours a day. There aren't "rules," per se, about what actions you HAVE to do to talk to God. But adopting these habits will provide the tools that help you grow that relationship.

No rules, just tools. (That may be my new favorite rhyme. You're welcome again.)

Journaling

This morning, I came home from my favorite store and sat down in my comfy chair to spend a little time with God. I'm not good at setting aside time every single day, but a few mornings a week I make time to sit and think and pray a bit.

Thanks to the iHome my parents gave me for Christmas, I scrolled my iPod to an old worship album from my college days and started to journal as the music played. I wrote about a guy I used to like and how he now has a new girlfriend (ouch). I wrote out some prayers for college students I know here in Nashville. I described some worries that keep flittering around the corners of my mind. I sat quietly and thought about things, picturing some situations I am in that I don't know how to handle. And I asked God, in my heart and with my pen, to teach me how to handle those situations well. How do I show love? How do I act with wisdom? How do I encourage?

I read some of 1 Peter, a book of the Bible written by our friend Peter. I just can't kick the connection I feel with that dude, and one of my all-time favorite verses about Jesus sits right on the first page of that book.

1 PETER 1:8-9

> Though you have not seen him, you love him; and even though you do not see him now, you believe in him and are filled with an inexpressible and glorious joy, for you are receiving the goal of your faith, the salvation of your souls.

I love it in *The Message* version too:

> You never saw him, yet you love him. You still don't
> see him, yet you trust him—with laughter and singing.
> Because you kept on believing, you'll get what you're
> looking forward to: total salvation.

Journaling is part of my life now, but it's a tool that I have
adopted and practiced and grown through. Sixteen years ago,
that wasn't the case.

The first journal I ever wrote in was given to me by my
small group leader the summer between my junior and senior
years of high school. She handed it to me the Sunday before our
church youth group went to the beach. I remember sitting on
the balcony of our cheap oceanfront hotel room and pondering
hard about how I wanted to start the journal.

I opened the beautiful journal—navy blue with gold and
white stars and moons and suns—and read Laurel's inscription.

> Annie,
>
> May your dreams and prayers reach beyond the sun,
> moon, and the stars.
>
> Here is a place for you to jot down your favorite
> Scripture, a dream, or just your thoughts.

And then she wrote some personal stuff about our friendship
and her prayers for me.

With those kind words and instructions, I was ready to get
started.

I'd had enough "diaries" in my life to know I didn't want

to start with "Dear Journal." I was making college choices and boy choices and grown-up decisions and my life at that point was much different from the one I'd captured in my middle-school diary.

This was serious business.

So I started with the date, the day of the week, and the location.

Then I just started to write, stream-of-consciousness style, about being at the beach, how it was my last summer on this retreat that had become a favorite, and about this cute new guy who had just come on the scene.

(In retrospect, that actually does sound a lot like a diary. But don't tell seventeen-year-old Annie that.)

And then I did something new for me. I wrote a prayer. I started to transcribe the words my head was praying to God about what college I should go to (University of Georgia or Samford University?) and my fears regarding my senior year of high school and all the many transitions that begin that year of life and stop, well, never (sorry to say).

I didn't know if I was doing it right, this journaling thing. I didn't know if there were rules that I hadn't read or if God expected something particular, I just know how I felt—peaceful. Quieted. I knew when I was done, my hand had slowed and my thoughts had as well. Everything felt calm, except the beach breeze blowing my hair across my face.

A lot of years and about fifteen journals later, I'm still going. Not every day; sometimes I will miss a week or two or a month, but I always have a journal sitting there, waiting on me to scratch my heart across its pages.

While I was writing this, I was hanging with two of the girls from my CrossPoint Church small group, talking about college and dudes and the Lent season and gal stuff. We were discussing our plans for small group that night and I mentioned, in passing, that the girls should bring their journals. To my utter shock, neither of them had a journal. It took me a minute to remember that they are not that much older now than I was when I began journaling.

And then I got all giggly, because one of the joys of leading a small group is introducing my girls to spiritual disciplines or life lessons or skillz that they may not already know. (Example: praying out loud, how to cook with a Crock-Pot, and so on. My favorite Crock-Pot recipe? In the appendix. Check it.)

So that night, when the girls arrived and we finished eating our taco soup, I pulled the huge clear plastic tub from the hallway closet and showed them my ever-growing collection of journals.

Every notebook I have written in, scribbled on, and cried over for the last sixteen years is stored in this container. I pulled out specific ones and told the girls about my memories from that season of life. How the one with the photograph of a little boy and girl in black and white was my freshman year of college and I accidentally left it at church one day and felt panicked because I wrote about my crush in there. How the one with the hand-drawn armor of God went along on the first mission trip I led. . And I showed them that first one, with the white and gold stars, not even halfway full, but so meaningful.

I read a few carefully selected excerpts to the girls, and I told them what to do with my journals when I die. (Burn them all. No reading them. Seriously.)

It was a sweet experience for our group—for them to see some of my history and for me to look back through some of those formative seasons of my life.

That's what journaling does. It records seasons. It holds questions and hurts and hopes and prayers from different times in your life.

I know not everyone loves writing, I get that. But I think journaling in some form or fashion is super important—whether that is a pen to paper, writing a song, making lists on your computer, writing a blog post, whatever. You need to journal to record God's faithfulness in your life. You need a place where important verses are collected. You need a spot where you hurt, then wrestle with God, and survive it. You need to write the prayers that seem to never get answered. You need to write the ones that do.

When it is so easy for me to forget how many times God has saved the day, or feel like He has forgotten me, I have my journals to remind me that He has always been there for me.

Prayer

Prayer is our most direct connection to God—your voice to His ear. I don't have any special insider information on prayer. I don't understand why it seems to "work" sometimes and then not work other times. I can list for you many prayers I have uttered throughout the years that I don't understand what God did with them.

We've talked about the power of prayer and, y'all, it is real. Praying changes things. But in this section, we aren't going to have a conversation about why God answers some prayers and seems to not answer others or why some people get healed and others don't. If your focus, or my focus, is on how God answers and why God answers, we've totally missed the purpose of prayer.

So why do we pray? What's the root of all of it? To get stuff? To change God's mind so He'll give us what we want?

We pray because it connects us to God and deepens that relationship.

When I was in the ninth and tenth grades, my best friend at school was named Chrissy. I loved getting to school because Chrissy and I would sit down and talk like crazy because it had been a full fourteen hours since we were in the same room. (This was in the ancient days before social media helped us to know what our friends are doing at any waking moment . . . and some sleeping moments.) I told her about soccer practice and whatever crazy my little sisters had gotten into, and she would tell me about cheerleading and the boy she liked and anything else of import.

We didn't talk because we had to or because we had a goal of growing our friendship. We never walked into homeroom thinking, "Today I shall speaketh to my friend in order that our friendship may flourish." Of course not. But I wanted her to know what was important to me because she was important to me.

That's why we pray.

Can we ask God for things? Certainly. I mean, not pots of gold at the end of a rainbow per se, but there is an element of prayer that is about telling God what we need and want and trusting Him to answer in a way that is best for us. I still pray for a husband, I pray for my friends to be healed, I pray for our president, I pray for financial provision for myself and for others I care about, like missionaries. So, totally—prayer can be asking for things.

But remember, God is not a vending machine in the sky or Amazon.com, or even the Starbucks drive thru. You can't place an order and expect it to be ready for you when you drive around the corner, piping hot with whipped cream.

Go into prayer with one main goal: growing your relationship with God. There is no greater gift, nothing you could ask for, that is better than knowing Him. The Bible says that one day in His courts is better than a thousand elsewhere (see Psalm 84:10).

Don't get me wrong—sometimes prayer absolutely changes things. You can read story after story in the Bible of how someone prayed and it altered the future. Healings. Freedom. Direction. All of it. And I've seen it in my life and the lives of my friends and family—over and over again. There is power in prayer.

But if we are talking about how we use our words, here's the truth: we use our words in prayer to get to know God better, not to get stuff that we want.

Don't know how to pray? Intimidated to start? I totally get that. I feel that way some days too. But Jesus modeled for us how to pray, and I use His example a lot to jump-start my prayer times.

MATTHEW 6:9-13

This, then, is how you should pray:

"Our Father in heaven, hallowed be your name,
your kingdom come, your will be done, on earth as it is in heaven.
Give us today our daily bread.
Forgive us our debts, as we also have forgiven our debtors.
And lead us not into temptation, but deliver us from the evil one."

So either out loud, or in my journal, it goes like this:

Our Father in heaven, hallowed be your name,

I think You're great, God. I worship You. Your name is holy.

your kingdom come, your will be done, on earth as it is in heaven.

Yeah, there are just some things going on, God, where I'm asking for You to step in—like my friend's dad being sick. I pray You would heal him, that Your will would be done. I'm also trying to decide about which project to take next—I want to do whatever is best, whatever is Your will. Will You reveal that to me?

Give us today our daily bread.

It's almost the end of the month and I'm just not sure I'm going to have enough money, God. But I trust You to provide for me. Please help me to have enough money to get through this last week.

Forgive us our debts, as we also have forgiven our debtors.

Ugh. This is hard for me today because I'm so mad at Susan and how she was talking bad about Karen. I just don't want to be nice to her or be around her. Forgive my hard heart. I know You've forgiven me—help me to forgive her.

And lead us not into temptation, but deliver us from the evil one.

God, it's super hard to stay away from temptation when it is ALL AROUND ME. Would You protect me? Show me the way out of tempting situations and how I can run the other direction.

So see? That five-line prayer gets a lot longer when it gets personal, when each line starts to mean something to you. It's not complicated, but it is life-changing.

Dear friend, I am barely going knee-deep into the realities of prayer. I know this feels surface-y and many of you wish we'd talk more about what prayer is and isn't and how to do it. First of

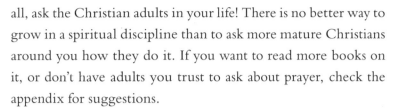

all, ask the Christian adults in your life! There is no better way to grow in a spiritual discipline than to ask more mature Christians around you how they do it. If you want to read more books on it, or don't have adults you trust to ask about prayer, check the appendix for suggestions.

The other way to get better at prayer? Practice. Just do it. Out loud in your car, quietly in your room, in your journal, at church, at school, with your friends and with your family. Just pray. Talk to God, telling Him the things that matter to you, the things you need, the things you feel.

Worship

I couldn't fall asleep last night. My yesterday was intense with radio interviews and teaching a class on writing, an important business meeting, and well, writing this book. When my head finally hit the pillow, it was like my mind sloshed all my thoughts around and nothing made sense anymore. I mentally made lists of things I needed to do and write and say and email and tweet, and I began to worry. Was my family okay? What if I handled that friendship situation wrong? AM I SCREWING UP MY ENTIRE LIFE?

Obviously, I'm very rational late into the night. (And by late, I mean 11 p.m. I'm crazy now that I'm in my thirties.)

So I got that trusty new iHome and started a favorite worship album. I crawled back under my winter stack of blankets and began to quietly sing along to the songs. And it is like my mind was being filled with new words, washing out the old ones.

That's what worship does, I think. It takes the focus off me and my issues and turns my attention to the One who can handle it all. To the One who deserves my focus.

It's true when people say that worship is a lifestyle—it is. But in this particular instance, our focus is worshiping with our words, and almost always that looks like worshiping in song.

I like to play worship music when I'm getting ready in the morning. It sets my mind right, it gives focus to my day, and it keeps me from crawling back into bed and going to sleep. (Also, I've started making my bed every morning so THAT keeps me from crawling back in as well.)

PSALM 59:16

I will sing of your strength, in the morning I will sing of your love; for you are my fortress, my refuge in times of trouble.

When it comes to using our words to speak love to God, nothing fits that better than worship. Sometimes other people say things way better than I ever could, and their songs become mantras that I believe about God or want to believe about God.

It doesn't matter the style you like—whether you rock hard or prefer piano music, whether a capella is your jam or it's full bands. What matters is that the words you sing resonate in your heart and head up to God.

In worship, we get to tell God how great He is. I heard a pastor talk recently about how the Bible teaches about the sacrifice of praise—how it doesn't always feel good to worship and tell God that He is great. I know that's true. There have been seasons of my life when I have barely been able to get the words out as the song played because my heart was broken or hurt or annoyed or questioning whether or not what I was saying was true.

When I look at my iTunes, one of the top-played songs is "All the Poor and Powerless" by All Sons & Daughters. The lyrics speak to my heart about who God is and how I want the world to know of Him. So I use my voice, as unimpressive as it is, to sing this song out to God.

When I was in high school, I had CDs by some of my favorite Christian artists—Point of Grace and Michael W. Smith were two faves. I didn't know that you could also have recordings of music we sang at church until the winter of my senior year, when I attended a retreat called In The Vine. There was a worship band there, and that first night after they played, as we left the auditorium, there was a table in the back with worship CDs.

I thought I had died and gone to heaven. You mean I can have the same songs we sing in church IN MY EARS ANYTIME I WANT?

I know. It sounds ridiculous now. But boy, it rocked my world. All Saturday during our retreat free time, I stayed in my top bunk with my earphones on, listening to worship songs over and over.

Now all we have to do is pop on YouTube and someone has probably put up a lyric video of your favorite song from Sunday morning worship or summer camp. The songs of worship are everywhere now.

Your voice rising to God is an atmosphere-changer. It changes the mood. It changes what is going on in the spiritual realm.

Also, it is a public thank-you. I don't tell God thanks enough. You probably don't either. But worship is a full-on thank-you fest. Whether or not you feel it—whether it has been the worst week of school or you just won a gold medal at the Olympics—worship overrides our emotions and lets us speak truth. Speak love.

(Looking for some great worship albums to purchase? Check the appendix, yo.)

One Last (Important) Thing

I know this chapter has been long. But in reality, if we aren't using our words well to speak to God, then none of our other relationships will work well either. I wanted to camp here, at the place that matters the most. He is the center, He's the core. So I'm okay that we had to push into this one a little more than some later chapters.

This is your priority. This is the river relationship from which all your words flow.

> **LUKE 6:45**
>
> Out of the overflow of [her] heart [her] mouth speaks.

I think that's why it is important for me to start my day talking to God. Don't get me wrong, I don't have a four-hour prayer/worship/journaling sesh every day (but if you do, I'm totally impressed and think that is great). When I wake up, at the suggestion of my friend Emily Freeman, I try to start my day listening. I whisper some hellos to God while my eyes adjust to the morning and my body stretches awake. And then I listen . . . Before I grab my iPhone and check my email and every other social media site on the globe, I try to make it about God.

If that's how I start, the rest of the day seems to have more purpose.

Your Words Matter

Memorize the Word

> I will sing of your strength, in the morning I will sing of your love; for you are my fortress, my refuge in times of trouble.
>
> —PSALM 59:16

Read the Word

- 1 Timothy 4:12
- 1 Peter 1:8–9
- Psalm 84:10
- Matthew 6:9–13
- Luke 6:45
- Read in Exodus about all the times that worship occurs—with Miriam, Moses, etc. (If you need help finding verses, use the keyword function on BibleGateway.com or page to the topical index in your Bible.) It's fascinating WHEN the people decided to worship and WHY.
- Use your concordance or BibleGateway.com to search these terms:
  - prayer, praying, prays
  - worship, praise, worshipers

Journal Your Words

- Write out a prayer of thanksgiving to God—tell Him the things you are thankful for today. Need help getting started? Write T-H-A-N-K-Y-O-U down the page of your journal and write one word or phrase for each letter about something you are thankful to God for.

- Have you ever considered writing a song about God? Start here! Write a poem sharing truths about who God is. (And then if you want to, grab your guitar or piano or your musically inclined BFF and turn it into a song!)
- When is the first time you remember God answering your prayers? Tell that story in your journal.
- List five situations in your life where you need God to answer your prayers.

Use Your Words

- You need a journal if you don't have one, sister. Whether that's a Word document on your computer or a blank book you found in your closet or pages ripped from an old school notebook and stapled together, you need a place to record what God is doing for you.
- Share a YouTube video of your favorite worship song on social media. Use the hashtag #SpeakLove so we can all see it!

PART 2

Conversations with Others

Each word or thought of yours can be like a pearl that you drop into the secret place of another heart, and in some hour of need, lo! the recipient finds the treasure and realizes for the first time its value.

—*GOD CALLING*, JANUARY 7

God isn't the only One who gets our words. Already today (by the way, it is 3 p.m.), I've talked out loud to my intern, my roommate, and the girl who works at the YMCA (because my account got cancelled, which I'm sure has nothing to do with the fact that I hadn't been to the gym in over a month). Also, the cute guy at the water fountain and I had a real heart-to-heart about who should go first filling up our water bottles. It went like this:

Him to me: "Go ahead."
Me to him: "Oh, you were here first are you sure you don't mind okay I'll hurry but really how can I hurry in this situation hahaha."
Him to me: ". . . "

So, obviously, the conversation meant a lot to him too.

Since returning from the gym, I've texted a few different friends and my mom, I've checked Twitter and Facebook too many times, and I've written on a few Facebook walls and tweeted about how I still wish I had worn my retainer. (Seriously, if you learn nothing else from this book, learn this: WEAR YOUR RETAINER. Your thirty-three-year-old self will thank you. Or have crooked teeth regrets, as I do.)

(That is not your cue to stare at my teeth next time we are in the same place, okay?)

This is a quiet day for me. I'm a talker and I love being around my people, because I love my people. I bet you love your people too. I bet they also make you crazy, angry, happy, sad, and every other emotion we could try to list here.

When it comes to speaking love, your people—even the ones you didn't choose to have in your life—are the ones most likely to be affected by how you are using your words. This verse comes back to my mind again:

LUKE 6:45

Out of the overflow of [her] heart [her] mouth speaks.

As we talked about in the last chapter, what comes out of your mouth is a direct reflection of what is going on in your heart.

I think of a few different categories when I think of the people you are speaking love to: your family (your parents and your siblings), other adults, your friends, the boys in your life, and—one of my favorite categories—celebrities you like a lot. (I think how we talk to celebrities online and when we meet them makes a bigger impression than you can imagine. We'll talk about it.)

As we proceed through this section, I want to remind you of what you already know: you don't have a perfect family or perfect friends (neither do I).

I don't know what it feels like to be you, but I do know what the Bible says, and so I want to present you with the truth and trust that the Holy Spirit in you is going to bring to life the areas where you need this reminder.

And listen. I know. This can be painful if your older brother has abused you and I'm going to tell you to be kind to him, or if your best friend stabbed you in the back and I'm going to tell you to focus on the good. Hang in there with me, let down your defenses, and go with me to these places. And when we're done, I hope you'll feel God near to you; He'll be your mouthpiece when you can't speak words of love on your own.

CHAPTER 5

Your Family

> Honor your father and your mother, as the Lord
> your God has commanded you, so that you may
> live long and that it may go well with you.
>
> —DEUTERONOMY 5:16

Family is a weird thing, isn't it? Some of you live in homes with a mom and a dad, and your older brother is the high school quarterback and your little sister is adorable twenty-four hours a day. For others, family is a painful topic, one laced with words like "abandonment" and "death" and "loneliness." Or you live with your grandparents. Or just your dad.

As for me? I have a mom and a dad and two younger sisters. Well, we actually have two other "sisters"—my cousins Jake and Julianne. For the last few years, these two cousins have spent more time with my parents than their own, including all holidays and pretty much any time we all go to dinner, so we consider them our sisters.

Yes, Jake is a boy, and yes, we call him our sister. And yes, we did make him wear footie pajamas one year on Christmas Eve, and yes, he was twenty-four years old. Julianne lived with my parents for the last two years of high school, and I'd like to publicly complain that she took my childhood bedroom. So for two whole years, every time I went to visit my parents, I had to sleep in the GUEST room. Phfff. Rude.

(Actually, it was fine and I totally love Julianne, so I'm not nearly as annoyed as I always told her I was. Hey, I'm the big sister. I gotta give her a little friendly trouble, right?)

So my family is both traditional and non-traditional. But you know what? I don't know that any of us would call our families "traditional," would we? Because your grandfather may live in the basement or you may be in a foster home. Maybe you were adopted, your parents are divorced, or you have seventeen siblings.

And while few of us would claim to have a traditional family, there is something sweet about the idea that we each know our own normal. I think my family is normal (except for the fact they are all weirdos), because that is the only family I have known.

My family gets the best and the worst versions of me—and I get the best and worst of them. When things are good, they are really good and we laugh and have a blast being together. When things aren't good, they are disastrous and people are hurt and crying and annoyed and . . . yikes.

I wish I could tell you that conflict goes away when you grow up, but it hasn't for us. Maturity has helped, calming our nerves and our tongues, but it hasn't removed our humanness.

As you already know from my all-too-public apology, my sisters (the two actual ones, not the cousin-sisters) are the VIPs of my angry words—Very Injured Persons. Hopefully that was more limited to my teen years and we're on the upside of it now.

It's tough to use your words well in your own home. I know. I get it. But that's our goal, that's our heart, as girls who want to speak love with our lives. So let's talk about the different ways we can really do that for the people we call our family.

Parents

I was never the kid who talked back to my parents. At least, not that I can remember. Maybe my parents would say different, but I was not the defiant type. I would get mad at them, sure—I had my moments—but I didn't tend to yell at them or say ugly things in general.

Instead, I hid my words from them. I concealed my worries and my struggles and my mistakes (or so I thought). I said what I thought was the right thing, not the true thing.

Don't get me wrong. I'm not saying I was a quiet and demure child or teenager who just sat where she was supposed to sit and did what she was supposed to do. Not at all, actually. I think I was a fairly major pain in the backside. Here was my issue (prepare yourself; it's weird).

I spent most of my young Christian life feeling like I had to earn people's love, including God's and my parents'. Also, I thought if I was going to be a "good Christian example" to my friends at school, I was not allowed to make mistakes or have any struggles in public. So I would work really, really hard to say and do the right thing anytime I was around my friends, because I felt pressure to behave in a way that I understood represented God best. (P.S.—that's not true. The best way to represent God to the world is to be YOU—on good days and bad. He is seen in your strengths but even better in your weaknesses.) Because I didn't grasp that, I ignored grace and focused on works.

Obviously, my life was really fun. No mistakes allowed and all love earned? It was a great time. (That's sarcastic, by the way.)

Because of this I worked very hard to be perfect at school. (Which is one reason I didn't always tell the truth—I didn't want to look like I ever made a mistake or had any issues.) So when I got home? That was my time to relax emotionally. I don't know if this makes any sense, but it is like I was performing all day long and my house was the only place I was allowed to be human, so BOY, WAS I HUMAN.

(If you relate to this at all, please read *Graceful: Letting Go of Your Try-Hard Life* by Emily P. Freeman. Wowsa, does she get teenage Annie.)

It wasn't that I was mean to my parents. It was just that I was a bit aloof most of the time. I wanted to rest and not have to be perfect. But I didn't want to be imperfect, because that gave them the chance to not love me. So I decided it was better to protect myself from that and pull back than to be fully invested in my family and risk being rejected.[1]

My words, how I spoke to my parents, had far more to do with me just wanting a break from the life of attempted perfection.

---

1   And no, my parents didn't tell me that I wasn't allowed to make mistakes or anything crazy like that—this was definitely all in my head. Though I am sure there are parents out there who inflict this type of pain on their kids (telling them that mistakes are not allowed), that was not my situation.

I think my parents were hurt by my withdrawal, but some families get hurt just as much by aggression and anger. I used to spend the night frequently at my best friend Connie's house. Her parents were divorced and honestly, in the five or so years that we were close, I don't ever remember meeting her dad. But I do clearly remember being so taken aback and frightened when she would scream (and I mean SCREAM) at her mother. She would say the most awful things, and, to be honest, her mom would too.

I'm not friends with Connie anymore. I've looked for her multiple times on social media and can't find her anywhere. But I wonder about how those words have affected their relationship now that she and her mom are both adults.

And listen, we could talk all day about how words from our parents have hurt us. I'm sure you could and I know I can. But the honest truth is that I still honor my parents and love them, so I don't want to write those stories.

Also, as we've talked about, this isn't a defensive book where we talk about all the ways that other people have used words to hurt us in our lives. Yes, how your parents speak to you does and will affect you. But in the end, that doesn't determine how you use YOUR words with them. If your parents are loving and cuddly and always tell you how totes adorbs you are, it is probably easier for you to use kind and loving words toward them. If your parents are mean and horrible and abusive, it is terribly difficult and you might be tempted to treat them and others the same way, or not even express your true feelings. I'm not discounting that pain at all.

But if you ask me, whether you refuse to bite your tongue or refuse to release it, both are sins. When you spit venom, you are sinning. When you deceive by withholding words, you are sinning. I wish we got to behave based on how others behave toward us, but unfortunately that's not the rules of this game called the Christian life.

(Having a great time yet? Stick with me.)

Check out this verse:

DEUTERONOMY 5:16

Honor your father and your mother, as the Lord your God has commanded you, so that you may live long and that it may go well with you.

Do you know what I love about this verse? It's the first of the Bible's Ten Commandments that has a promise attached. Unfortunately, it doesn't also have a caveat attached that says, "If your parents are awesome and perfect . . ." Instead, God puts it to us straight.

How you treat your parents says a lot about who you are AND who you will become. If you can attempt to be loving with your words, honoring your parents in your decision making and in your life, God promises that it will go well for you.

Does that mean rainbows and unicorns and Easter-shaped candies in your every day? I wish, but no. It just means that life will be better if you can find a way to speak love to your parents.

(Do I need to say again how much I KNOW THIS ISN'T EASY FOR EVERYONE? I know. I hope you know that I know. But again, it doesn't change what the Bible says, y'all. It just doesn't.)

And if you don't live with your parents, but have another day-to-day authority figure God has placed in your life who fills the role of "parent," this applies to you too.

What does it look like to honor your parents, particularly with your words? Here are a few examples:

- Share honestly, yet calmly, when you disagree with them.
- Tell them "thank you" when they buy you something or take you somewhere.
- Bring up fun memories of the past.
- Put your phone away when your parents are talking to you.
- Be respectful of your parents in front of other people as well as at home.
- Speak kindly about them on social media; even if you are mad, don't use the Internet to air your family's issues.
- Write an encouraging note to your mom or dad—it doesn't have to be long, just a sticky note saying one thing you love about them or a Bible verse that you are praying for your parent.
- PRAY FOR YOUR PARENTS.

And please remember—before they were your parents, and even now, they were and still are two humans who grew up and fell in love and have been hurt and have had both amazing days and heartbreaking ones. They have issues and baggage and memories that you may never know but may affect you every day. You don't need to earn their love by being perfect, just like they don't need the pressure from you to be perfect either. Be full of grace with them, on the good days and the bad.

Sibling Stuff

(FYI: I know that there are some only children out there. Even if you aren't a sister yourself, can I suggest you read this section anyway? You might soon mentor a young woman who needs help being a better sister, or when you grow up, you might be a mom who will need to raise your kids to treat each other well. So don't skip over this just because you aren't a sister. Check out 1 Timothy 5:1–2.)

Before we talk about what to say to your siblings, let's talk about why we have them.

I don't know.

I don't know exactly why God made it so that multiple people come from the same parents. But from the first parents, Adam and Eve, there were siblings. And those first ones? Yikes. Not so good. If you read Genesis 4, you will see that the first brothers ever to exist on earth didn't get along. In fact, the older brother ended up murdering the younger one. Whoa.

So it's been a struggle from the beginning, if that makes you feel any better.

And while I don't know why, I think God made siblings because:

- it's nice to have someone else who has grown up under the same roof as you
- they are some of the only friends you will likely have for your entire life
- siblings make you the most crazy, but they also can be the best practice for learning to love someone on the hard days

And honestly, those are just my guesses. God does a lot of stuff that I don't totally understand but appreciate. Like giraffes and watermelons.

Whether or not you believe it today, your siblings are a gift. Whether they are the kind of gift that makes your life a better place or the kind of gift that makes you trust God more, God made your family and gave you those exact brothers and/ or sisters. They aren't perfect, and in some cases they are really unkind. I know that. As you've heard me say before (and I'm sure it made you crazy then too), we unfortunately don't get to decide how we speak based on how other people speak to us. So your job is to use your words well to be the best sister you can be.

We could spend a whole book talking about sisters in the Bible and how they used their words. Instead, I've simplified it for you a little bit. When I look at these sisters, certain things jump out at me about how they acted, how they used their words. These examples give me a chance to choose—Do I react how I WANT to or react how I NEED to?

While the women in the Bible are also flawed (Jesus is the only perfect person), they give us good stories and reminders of what kind of sisters we want to be.

Be a supportive sister.

Miriam was Moses's sister. You can read about her in Exodus 2.

When he, as a tiny baby, was put in a basket and sailed down the river to Pharaoh's house, it was Miriam who followed the basket full of brother and then spoke up to Pharaoh's daughter when she was looking for someone to nurse the baby. Miriam's words made a way for her and her mom to take care of Moses while he was still an infant.

As Moses grew up, Miriam was constantly by his side as a support. My favorite story is in Exodus 15 when Moses led the Israelites in a song and then Miriam picked up and led the women in a chorus. Living in Nashville, I get lots of opportunities to hear people sing songs they wrote, and nothing makes a songwriter feel more supported than when others join in and sing along. I think that must have been really encouraging for Moses—there he was, leading the people in life and in song, and his sister joins in and leads the women to follow Moses and God as well.

That's who we are to be as sisters. Our words should support our siblings in their dreams and their plans.

(Also, I think it is worth noting that in Numbers 12, Miriam gossips and speaks against Moses and gets in A LOT of trouble with God. Check it out.)

Be an honest sister.

When Lazarus died, his sister Martha saw Jesus first and then went to get his other sister, Mary, to bring her to Jesus as well. While they were both hurting, they were honest when they talked to Jesus about Lazarus. Another interesting thing to note is that they were honest in front of each other. Nothing will bring down walls of pride between sisters like grief. And Jesus.

How weird is this—both sisters said the same thing to Jesus right when they saw Him.

JOHN 11:21

"Lord," Martha said to Jesus, "if you had been here, my brother would not have died."

JOHN 11:32

When Mary reached the place where Jesus was and saw him, she fell at his feet and said, "Lord, if you had been here, my brother would not have died."

Don't you think that is interesting? They both are expressing their grief about their brother's death while also saying to Jesus that they know He is God. They are honest, and that's how we should speak about our siblings and to our siblings.

Be a Jesus-focused sister.

In this same situation, when Lazarus has died, remember Martha runs back to the house and gets Mary. To get the fullness of this story, let's pick up mid-convo between Martha and Jesus, before Martha heads back to the house to retrieve Mary.

> ### JOHN 11:25–29
>
> Jesus said to her, "I am the resurrection and the life. He who believes in me will live, even though he dies; and whoever lives and believes in me will never die. Do you believe this?"
>
> "Yes, Lord," she told him, "I believe that you are the Christ, the Son of God, who was to come into the world."
>
> And after she had said this, she went back and called her sister Mary aside. "The Teacher is here," she said, "and is asking for you." When Mary heard this, she got up quickly and went to him.

"The Teacher is asking for you," she said. A mean sister would have never told the little sister that Jesus was looking for her. But Martha used her words to point her sister toward Him, didn't she? We've seen Mary and Martha not get along before (like in Luke 10:38–42), so it's not that they are perfect sibling examples. But in the big moments, they remember what we should remember: your siblings may make you crazy, but they are your people. While you and I may not have the chance on this earth to physically escort someone to Jesus, we can do it with our words and our lives. You have the chance to speak in such a way that your siblings step toward Jesus.

Be a loving sister.

When I was in middle school, my mom made me write this next verse one hundred times. Seriously. ONE HUNDRED. I remember sitting at my little white wooden desk and furiously writing it.

> **1 JOHN 4:20**
>
> If anyone says, "I love God," yet hates his brother, he is a liar. For anyone who does not love his brother, whom he has seen, cannot love God, whom he has not seen.

Yes, I know this version says "brother." Trust me, I argued that exact point with my mother all those years ago. "MOM, I DO NOT *HAVE* A BROTHER, SO HOW CAN I HATE SOMEONE I DON'T *HAVE*?!?" Yeah, like I said, I was a real pleasure. (This is one of the times when I actually do remember getting mad enough to yell at my parents.)

We are called to be loving. You might say, "Yeah, I totally love my little brother" or "Of course I love my older sister." But if I was to ask THEM, would I get the same answer? Would they say your words reflect your heart?

Or, here's something that gives a yucky feeling but something I realized used to be true of me (and sometimes still is): do your words reveal slimy, ugly ick in your heart?

I know. I hate that too.

Our truest selves are revealed when we are with our families. But here's the beautiful thing about that—it doesn't take much for Jesus to change your family through you. Have you been awful in the past? You can apologize, in person or in a letter, or just make a change. Ask God to forgive you for using your words as weapons and ask Him to teach you how to speak love to the people in your family. As much as that verse made me crazy when I had to write it one hundred times, it is still true. How can we claim to love God if we don't love our family?

It's not easy. I'm still not always good at it. But I know this—I want my family to love Jesus more because of my life, not in spite of me. And I want my words to help with that desire, not hurt it.

You can too, friend. You can use your words to bring life to your home. I know you can. Just try tomorrow. Say the kind thing when the ugly comes to the surface, hold your tongue when you could yell, bless when you could curse. No, it's not some magic spell that is going to change everything in your home forever, but I bet your tomorrow will be different.

Try it.

Your Words Matter

Memorize the Word

> Honor your father and your mother, as the Lord your God has commanded you, so that you may live long and that it may go well with you.
>
> —DEUTERONOMY 5:16

Read the Word

- Luke 6:45
- Deuteronomy 5:16
- Exodus 2
- Exodus 15
- Numbers 12
- John 11
- Use your concordance or BibleGateway.com to search these terms:
  - ⊙ parent, parents, father, mother
  - ⊙ brother, sister
  - ⊙ family

Journal Your Words

- Write the memory verse in your journal.[2] Writing always helps me to actually memorize the Scripture quicker.
- Which family member do you find it most difficult to love with your words?
- Which member of your family sets a great example for you in how to use your words?
- Why is it hard to speak love at home?
- Write out a prayer, asking God to forgive you for how you have wrongly used your words toward your family in the past. Then ask Him to lead you in the future.

---

2   Just maybe not a hundred times . . .

Use Your Words

- Simply tell your family how much you love them. Send a note, write on each of their Facebook walls, or compliment your dad's tie, your mom's cooking, or your sister's cheerleading moves.
- Take the One Day Challenge—can you make tomorrow a day when you only speak love to your family? Just try it!

CHAPTER 6

Your People

Pleasant words are a honeycomb, sweet to the soul and healing to the bones,

—PROVERBS 16:24

You know, I've told you—I love my people. It is a unique love that you have with your family—a love that you never chose but get to feel and experience anyway. Your friends? You get to pick them. I think that is why now, as an adult, I love my friends' kids so much. They are these tiny versions of the people I picked to have in my life already!

So how we speak to them, all the people, matters. Your words matter.

I hope you're getting the idea that I'm putting across here—there is not a person in your world who is not affected by how you use your words. Your mom. Your best friend. Your best friend's mom.

I'm simply taking a minute to offer you an important reminder: You have power. Do you realize that sound waves, once they start, NEVER stop? That's science a friend shared with me and research has proved true. Your words? The ripple effects from those sounds continue on and on and on.

I love glitter. I like to say that it is my favorite color. Glitter. Confetti. Sequins. I love it all. I saw Katy Perry's movie *Part of Me* and I learned a lot from it (something we can talk about at another time), but my biggest takeaway?

I want a confetti cannon.

She has this tubular contraption she uses during her show to shoot confetti out into the crowd. It's like a T-shirt gun except it is full of tiny pieces of paper that cause a party anywhere they land.

I want one in my life. I want to have it with me every day. Can you imagine walking into a meeting and being like, "Sorry I'm five minutes late . . ." BOOM! You pull the trigger and fill the room with confetti. Or at the end of worship team practice at church, you say, "Great job, guys!" BOOM! A party breaks out because you have exploded joy across the room.

Without being too cheesy, I have to be honest and say that you get the chance to speak life like that—explode it onto the people who are in your life. The world is going to work hard to give you opportunities to kill relationships with words, because that is what Satan does—he kills, steals, and destroys (see John 10:10).

Words can do that, can't they? Man, I had one friendship with another girl that broke beyond repair simply because of words that were said. Ugly, ugly, ugly.

Words kill.

But the beautiful side? Words give life. And how you talk to the people in your life can build them up or tear them down. While both are going to happen (yes, you have permission to be human and mess up sometimes), your goal, *my* goal, is to work hard to love well with our words.

So while we've already covered our families (not in confetti—just meaning we've already discussed them), let's talk about the other people who live in our every day.

The Boss of You

What other adults are important in your life besides your parents? Maybe . . .

- grandparents
- teachers
- coaches
- youth leader
- small group leader
- Girl Scouts leader
- mentor
- me . . .

Okay, not really "me," besides in my writing or if you come hear me speak, unless you are one of the twelve college girls in my small group. But there are lots of other adults in your life who are invested in you and care about you. Whether you know it or believe it, it is true.

I used to coach high school soccer, and I remember thinking often of what a huge responsibility that was—not just to make sure the girls were in top running condition or knew how to handle a corner kick. Coaches get to invest in the lives of their players. About a week ago, one of my players emailed me a picture of a card I wrote in and sent to her probably nine years ago, and all her email said was, "I still think about you and am grateful for you." As a former coach, it meant so much that she even remembers my name. I spoke words of life to her all those years ago, but you know what? Last week, she spoke words of life to me as well.

You cannot overestimate how much your words will affect the adults in your life. You think it is no big deal to email an old soccer coach and say that? It absolutely marked my heart. You think your youth leader at church doesn't need to hear the story of how his talk last Sunday really changed how you view missions? I bet he does.

Last April, before my small group went home from college for the summer, we had a spend-the-night party. We call these get-togethers a "Small Group Snoozle." On the last class day of the semester, the crew of gals crashes at my place and we eat unhealthy-ish food and paint our nails and watch movies and pretty much just have a really great time until I head to my bedroom and let them sort out which part of the floor they will claim for the night.

When they all arrived at this party, I had them write their home address on five envelopes apiece and then we put those envelopes in a bowl and mixed them all up. The bowl was passed around the room and each girl then drew out five different envelopes with five different addresses on them. Their assignment for the summer (yes, I give summer assignments) was to write notes to five girls in our group.

Each girl would write five notes over the summer and each girl would receive five notes over the summer.

Do you know what that meant?

That meant that I got to write and send five notes BUT I also got to receive five encouraging notes in the mail. As each of them arrived, I was absolutely thrilled. The girls took time to write the kindest things about what Tuesday nights had grown to mean to them and how God had done work in their hearts through our group.

On the days when I'm tired or frustrated with being a leader, I can look at those notes and remember why I do what I do.

I love the stories in the Bible where students honor their teachers. There is a simple and beautiful story in 1 Samuel 3 about the little boy, Samuel, and his boss, Eli the priest. Samuel's mother, Hannah, had given Samuel to the house of the Lord to be raised as a priest. You can read all about that in 1 Samuel 1–2. In chapter 3, Samuel is in his room going to bed and Eli is in his room, and Samuel hears a voice calling to him.

1 SAMUEL 3:1-9 (THE MESSAGE)

The boy Samuel was serving God under Eli's direction. This was at a time when the revelation of God was rarely heard or seen. One night Eli was sound asleep (his eyesight was very bad—he could hardly see). It was well before dawn; the sanctuary lamp was still burning. Samuel was still in bed in the Temple of God, where the Chest of God rested.

Then God called out, "Samuel, Samuel!"

Samuel answered, "Yes? I'm here." Then he ran to Eli saying, "I heard you call. Here I am."

> Eli said, "I didn't call you. Go back to bed." And so he did.
>
> God called again, "Samuel, Samuel!"
>
> Samuel got up and went to Eli, "I heard you call. Here I am."
>
> Again Eli said, "Son, I didn't call you. Go back to bed." (This all happened before Samuel knew God for himself. It was before the revelation of God had been given to him personally.)
>
> God called again, "Samuel!"—the third time! Yet again Samuel got up and went to Eli, "Yes? I heard you call me. Here I am."
>
> That's when it dawned on Eli that God was calling the boy. So Eli directed Samuel, "Go back and lie down. If the voice calls again, say, 'Speak, God. I'm your servant, ready to listen.'" Samuel returned to his bed.

I know it is simple. But do you see that three times Samuel hopped up when he thought Eli was calling him? And Eli always answered with kindness. And what about Samuel? When I was a teenager, I wasn't so polite when my mom woke me up for school—I can't imagine thinking I heard her three times in the middle of the night, waking up and going to check only to find her still sleeping. I would have been annoyed. Samuel was fine with it.

As you continue to read in chapter 3, check out verse 19.

1 SAMUEL 3:19

> The Lord was with Samuel as he grew up, and he let none of his words fall to the ground.

Samuel honored his authority figures, and in turn God honored him. And later Samuel became the authority figure for King David. How David responded to Samuel left a mark forever in the history of Israel and the world. (Read 1 Samuel 16.)

Remember that we are always speaking life or death (see Proverbs 18:21) and you get the chance to speak life to the adults in your world. Here are some examples (though I'm sure you can think of tons of other ways to use your words well for them):

- Write an encouraging post on their Facebook wall.
- Send a letter in the mail.
- As you leave class, just thank your teacher. "Thanks for today, I enjoyed class." That's it. No biggie.

My favorite teacher was my third-grade teacher, Mrs. Albers. I can't tell you all the reasons why; I guess I don't remember. I just knew she was the best. She was fun, loved being around us, and made me feel like school was going to be awesome every day. In fact, I think that year was when I decided that I wanted to teach school when I was an adult.

When I was in college, I found Mrs. Albers's email address on the elementary school website and emailed her. I happily told her with my adult words all the ways she had nurtured my child heart. She wrote back, equally as happy to hear from me.

You don't have to wait years to tell an important adult in your life how much they've meant to you. One of my best friends is Kathleen. She's a good fifteen years older than me—in fact, all through middle and high school, she led my small group. So she put up with a pretty difficult version of Annie. Now as an adult, I love talking with her. No, I don't tell her every time we talk how much she means to me, but I've said it. And I'll say it again. (And I'm writing about her here—HI, KATHLEEN!!) But I speak love to her just in our friendship, in the things we talk about and in how we share life. Also, she makes these killer desserts that are banana and peanut butter and white chocolate quesadillas, and desserts with white chocolate are pretty much my love language. So that's the other reason I keep her around. (Just kidding, Kathleen.)

It's not hard to love the adults who have invested in you. You feel it in their friendship—that they care, that they aren't quitting you, that they are proud of you. But it is sometimes hard to express that appreciation. But go for it—I promise, you will confetti cannon joy into their whole day.

Also, let me note before we move on, there is a lot of hard in being a leader and a lot of heart in being a mentor. You can never know all that the adults in your life are dealing with. Plato is believed to have once said, "Be kind, for everyone you meet is fighting a great battle." So please just let me remind you—while your leaders (and parents) may look strong, they are battling. Everyone is. And kind words go a long way.

Friends: an Open Ear, a Closed Mouth

I can't quit thinking about the book of James. When it comes to how I speak to and about my friends, these verses seem to be the ones that stand out to me the most.

JAMES 3:3–12 (**THE MESSAGE**)

A bit in the mouth of a horse controls the whole horse. A small rudder on a huge ship in the hands of a skilled captain sets a course in the face of the strongest winds. A word out of your mouth may seem of no account, but it can accomplish nearly anything—or destroy it!

It only takes a spark, remember, to set off a forest fire. A careless or wrongly placed word out of your mouth can do that. By our speech we can ruin the world, turn harmony to chaos, throw mud on a reputation, send the whole world up in smoke and go up in smoke with it, smoke right from the pit of hell.

This is scary: You can tame a tiger, but you can't tame a tongue—it's never been done. The tongue runs wild, a wanton killer. With our tongues we bless God our Father; with the same tongues we curse the very men and women he made in his image. Curses and blessings out of the same mouth!

My friends, this can't go on. A spring doesn't gush fresh water one day and brackish the next, does it? Apple trees don't bear strawberries, do they? Raspberry bushes don't bear apples, do they? You're not going to dip into a polluted mud hole and get a cup of clear, cool water, are you?

You aren't new at being a girl. And I'm surely not the first to tell you how to use your words when you are talking with your friends. But I think this portion of Scripture is so valuable when we think about our friendships—how we talk to and about our friends.

I don't think anyone, not even my family, can cause me to be as two-faced (two-mouthed?) as my friends have historically. I spent so much time in middle school and high school praying intensely for my friends to become believers while also cussing occasionally and gossiping and not always telling the truth.

Brackish. Fresh water. Brackish. Brackish. Brackish.

It doesn't work.

Can I just say this to you? Stay away from gossip. Just do.

Here's the problem with gossip that somehow, even though I am a full-on adult, I still forget sometimes. Gossip has this way of deceiving us into believing that we have better and more trust-worthy friends, when in reality it is showing you which of your friends cannot be trusted. If they are talking with YOU about HER, they are talking with HER about YOU, just like you are probably talking with HER about THEM.

The ugly truth is that the friends who gossip, who are the center of the know-a-lot-and-tell-a-lot world, are the ones who get left out when things get hard. When the deep things are going on inside your soul, the gossips aren't the ones you're going to talk to. They hear only the surface stories because you know that they will tell.

I've been her. The girl on the inside who always was in the know, and you know what? I actually didn't like it. Sure, in the moment when someone wanted something juicy and I had it to give, rad. But when it came to the important stuff, I knew nothing. And I knew I knew nothing.

So I changed. And now I am the one who knows which friends don't get my stories and which friends can be trusted.

Be the one who can be trusted. Be the one who has an open ear, encouraging words, and a closed mouth.

On the other hand, when's the last time you took an extra minute to tell your girlfriends how great they are? My friend Rachael did the coolest thing on her birthday a few years ago. When we arrived at her home for a birthday brunch, there were cards by the door, each with one of our names on it—probably thirty envelopes total. In it, Rachael, on HER birthday, had written us each a note saying why she was grateful for us. I was so blessed by it that I adopted the idea myself. I love the opportunity to thank my friends for their love and kindness.

Think of Proverbs 16:24:

Pleasant words are a honeycomb, sweet to the soul and healing to the bones.

(Also, let's memorize that one. It's a good verse to have pop into your mind.)

If you want a list of what it looks like to use your words well with your friends, here we go:

1. Don't gossip.
2. Go out of your way to be kind.
3. Fight fair. Think before you speak.
4. Don't drop bombs in arguments that will prevent y'all from ever recovering. (You know the ones I mean—those comments you know are danger as soon as they come to your mind. Let it go. Don't say the thing you will regret.)
5. In every circumstance, be on your friends' team.
6. If someone else is talking bad about your friend, say something nice. If she is down on herself, say something true and kind. Something our small group used to say to each other all the time was, "I am FOR you." In every situation, even on the bad days, I am FOR my friends.
7. Don't gossip!

The best thing for us to do is remember how it feels when

awful words are used *toward us*. I have long said that I would rather learn to control my tongue by being on the receiving end of horrible words than on the giving end (though I have been there too). I have been in some pretty gnarly friend-fights in my life—two come to mind—where I know that the other person regrets the things she said and I was hurt badly. I don't ever want to do that to anyone else. Jesus would never do that to me.

Boys

Ah. The fellas.

I'll tell ya, I don't always know how to talk to boys. They are an interesting species that I wish I understood better. Truly. They think so differently than we do, they hear sentences differently than we say them, and they communicate in different ways than girls.

The truth? They are way simpler than we are, I think. Not stupid—don't hear me wrong. But when I ponder for twenty minutes what a text message means when the boy says, "How's your day?" he is probably just asking how my day is going, not wondering any of the other twelve questions I *think* he means.

Right? Right.

There are a lot of male options in your life. (And just to note, we are only talking about boys around your own age. There is never a time when an authority figure—a teacher, a coach, a leader—should be in one of these categories where you are trying to figure out what your emotions mean. If a grown man in your life is flirting or saying things that make you feel like he is interested in you in THAT way, you need to tell another adult, not figure out how to handle it yourself. Please? Okay? Thanks.)

So here are the categories of dudes that come to my mind:

- He's in your family.
- He's a friend, and that is it. You definitely don't and won't like him. No way.
- He's a friend, but he's in another relationship, so whether or not you would like him doesn't matter.
- He's a friend, but you could maybe like him.
- He's a friend, but you totally like him.
- You like him, but he doesn't know you exist.
- You like him, but you don't think he likes you.
- You like him, and he likes you.
- He's new to your world—you don't yet know what category he's going to fit into.

Phew. Maybe you can think of other categories, but I've gone through the address book on my phone and every single, age-appropriate unmarried guy fits into one of these categories. And to be honest, it really opened my eyes to a few situations I may not be paying enough attention to. ☺

So what I am saying is that boys are somewhat uncomplicated, girls are complicated, and our categories are complicated.

Nonetheless, we are lucky to have our guy friends and men in the world. It's okay to have guy friends—in fact, I think it is great! Jesus had friends who were girls and didn't cross boundaries, so we can do the same. Do I think a guy needs to be your number-one total bestie in the world? Nope. But I think it is healthy to have friends who are guys and friends who are girls. While both men and women are created in the image of God, we are able to see things about God in guys that we can learn from and appreciate.

And how we speak to them should reflect that truth. They are made in the image of God just like us, and just like us, words can build them up or tear them down.

Here come some basic *dude dos and don'ts* when it comes to how you use your words. Of course, there are more thoughts about all of this, and that's why it is important to have your parents or other godly adults in your life to help guide you. These are just guidelines, not rules. Let the people who know and love you help you do this well.

Think before you speak.

This is true in, well, every relationship. But I find with guys that if I think before I speak, I get myself in WAY less trouble. Just last week I made a joke to a guy about him being single on Valentine's Day, forgetting that he's not exactly over the breakup that he went through in the fall. Had I thought first, I would have never said it. It didn't build him up. It hurt his feelings and I had to apologize. Think first, girls, and you will save yourself a lot of apologies or embarrassing moments.

Don't call him a girl / princess / feminine descriptor.

He's not. He's a boy. Our job as girls who are choosing to speak love is to encourage strength in people and respect them. Remember, it is God's kindness that leads to repentance (Romans 2:4), not His anger or criticism that makes us want to change our behavior. No guy is going to act more manly because you call him a "wimp" or a "girl" or "girly." Stop being mean. It's not godly and, honestly, it isn't going to grow your friendship with that guy at all. Encourage his strengths.

Pray for him.

For sure. Pray for guys just like you pray for your girlfriends and leaders and other humans. But do so with this tiny caution: praying for people does something inside your heart—it connects you to them and makes you think about them more. That's not always a bad thing, but there have been times when I wanted to pray for a guy I cared about, but knew I needed to guard my heart because I didn't want to be thinking about him all day every day. Speaking of . . .

Guard your heart. And your stories.

Not everyone deserves to hear your hopes and dreams. Don't give them away. Just because he is your good friend doesn't mean he needs to hear what you want your life at thirty to be like. I always thought that when the Bible says to guard your heart (see Proverbs 4:23), it was more about keeping your mind pure sexually or not daydreaming about a wedding. But it is also about guarding the things that are IN your heart—your hopes, your dreams, your plans, and your worries. Guard them. Your girlfriends are good for sharing those things, and the man you are going to marry will be good when the time comes, also your parents or other godly leaders will be great ears. But sometimes, we should be like Mary in Luke 2:19 and just treasure up some things and keep them to ourselves, in our heart.

Use your words.

It's okay to tell a guy you think he is great or to celebrate him when he hits a homerun. While boundaries are a good thing (see Psalm 16:6), being open and honest and loving are good too. The more you practice using your words to speak life, the better you will understand where that boundary is for you in every relationship. I have lots of different guys in my life—college baseball players who are like little brothers, single guys I could maybe date someday, guys who are married to my friends—and every relationship has a different boundary on how I use my words. But I use them. And I learn. And I make mistakes. And I try again.

I always say I would rather go down encouraging someone than having a heart full of words I never said. So I tell you that and ask that you will take that sentence and mix it in a bowl full of *think before you speak* and *guard your heart* with a heavy scoop of wisdom and bake it in the oven. When it comes out, use those words to honor, support, and lift up the guys in your life.

Guys battle in ways we'll never understand, similar to how we battle in ways they can't know. But there is a beautiful place where we both respect each other's battles and speak life into the wounded places.

Be the girl who speaks life. Not the one who wounds.

All the folks we've talked about in this chapter are just people—humans doing the best they can to do this life and to handle the highs and lows. What a beautiful gift it is to use our words to make them stronger, braver, kinder, and lovelier.

We touched on how to be kind to friends, but I know there

is a deeper conversation here—about how friends can be awful, and what it feels like to get picked on, and how to stand up for yourself and your friends. Wait for it. The entire next chapter is on her. Her? Yeah, her. The mean girl.

Your Words Matter

Memorize the Word

> Pleasant words are a honeycomb, sweet to the soul and healing to the bones.
>
> **—PROVERBS 16:24**

Read the Word

- John 10:10
- 1 Samuel 1–3
- 1 Samuel 16
- Proverbs 18:21
- Romans 2:42
- Proverbs 4:23
- Psalm 16:6

Journal Your Words

- Write Proverbs 4:23 in your journal and list out some ways that you need God's wisdom when it comes to being open and generous with your words while also guarding your heart.
- List out EVERY person besides family who matters to you. Write them in your journal, and whether it is two people or twenty, write one positive word about each of

them and thank God for them. Use this list as a reminder of who to pray for.

Use Your Words

- Use them!
- Send a note to a leader in your life who has really touched your heart.
- Get a stack of sticky notes and cover your best friend's room with encouraging words and verses.
- Be your friends' biggest cheerleader! Whether for girls or boys, use your words in such a way that you are known as the girl who is ALWAYS on their side.

CHAPTER 7

The Mean Girl

> Confess your sins to each other and pray for
> each other so that you may be healed. The
> prayer of a righteous [person] is powerful and
> effective.
>
> —JAMES 5:16

Things are about to get serious up in here.

Because let me tell you something I don't have a lot of time for: people being mean. I think life is too short and words are too powerful for us to pretend like being brats is an okay thing.

Here are a few things all my friends know about me:

1. I'm habitually on time.
2. I'd rather be wearing a sweatshirt and jeans (if I'm not).
3. I'm going to invite too many people to every social event unless someone wisely limits me.

4. If I have on workout clothes, that does NOT necessarily indicate I am going to the gym.

5. I have a justice streak a mile wide.

What does that last one mean? It means if you hurt one of my friends, I'm going to be slow to get over it. It's not always a strength and it's not always a weakness. It is a part of me that I have to tame or let loose, depending on what God's wisdom would have me do in a situation.

My best friend Lyndsay says that my justice streak is fun to watch. Hurt my feelings? I'll get over it. Hurt one of my people's feelings? Break up with them? Be rude to them? I don't handle it as well. I get this serious look on my face, and I can feel my eyebrows raising, causing my forehead to wrinkle in a way it only wrinkles when I'm mad.

It's like my whole face is saying, "Excuse me? You did WHAT?"

I don't hit people (duh). I don't even scream or yell or often say the things I want to—but that is only because of years of living with this side of my personality and knowing that I have to hold my tongue.

And all that practice was put into action not long ago.

One of the best parts of my life is the Girls of Grace events that I am currently speaking for. We get to meet thousands of girls every weekend and I absolutely love it. A few months ago, we were at an event up north and as I was walking down the concourse (that's the fancy name for where all the merchandise tables are), a mom stopped me.

"Annie Downs?" she said.

"Yes ma'am?" I answered. For some reason, I was sure I was getting in trouble because

- she was a mom and
- she used my first and last name.

"Thank you for what you said in your talk about bullying." I had only mentioned that we should be using our words to be kind to each other. "You're welcome," I started to say, but before the words were out of my mouth she was continuing, "My daughter is here . . . and so is the girl who bullies her."

Well. I could feel my eyebrows going up and my forehead wrinkling.

"In this building?"

"Yes."

Well. I wanted to say next, "Get that girl to ME." And I was ready to use my teacher voice with a little growl on the side and give her a piece of my mind. But knowing that probably would somehow end up on Twitter or Instagram, I resisted. I just told the mom that I would be praying and to tell her daughter I'd like to meet HER.

You know why this mom's comment fired me up so quickly?

Because that was a building full of Christian girls. CHRISTIAN GIRLS. The ones who have God living inside of them would bully each other? I couldn't believe it.

But I could.

So. Here's what I did. Because—oh, don't you worry about it—I still dealt with that girl.

I just dealt with her from the stage.

About two hours later I was back on stage doing a Q&A with the rest of the speakers and musicians. I sat between our stylist,

Amber Lehman, and the amazing singer Britt Nicole. A question was posed to me about bullying, and I was ready.

I told them exactly what I'm going to tell you about the mean girl, except you don't have to see my furrowed brow. (But picture it, okay? Okay.)

The mean girl is hurting too. That's the real truth. The mean girl does what she does because she is trying to figure out a way to make herself feel better.

It's like when someone sees a grease fire and thinks the right answer is water (it isn't). They are just trying to put out the fire any way they can, not realizing that they are actually increasing the flames. (Do you know how to put out a grease fire? Check the appendix. It's good info to have.)

That's how bullying works, if you were looking for the science behind it. It's like the mean girl—whom we'll label the bully in our conversations—is burning like a grease fire and she thinks belittling other people will put out the fire of hurt inside of her. Instead, like adding water to the fire, it makes it worse and the flames of hurt lick up at her heart and mind all day.

She'll never tell you that. She'll never admit that she is hurting or that making you feel worse only makes her feel better in the minute and then goes away. She won't tell you that. But listen, it is true.

So I sat on that stage, with the microphone in my hand, and I said that.

And then I spoke straight to the mean girl. And if I'd known which girl that mom was speaking about, I probably would have walked out into the crowd and stood there, with my microphone, right beside her chair.

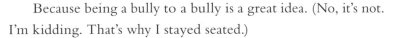

Because being a bully to a bully is a great idea. (No, it's not. I'm kidding. That's why I stayed seated.)

I told the mean girl that she had to stop. Now. That abusing other people because you are hurt is always wrong. I told her that she was going to lose in the end so she might as well quit now.

And I'm telling you too.

Are you the mean girl? Are you the victim? Or are you the girl who watches the mean girl and the victim and doesn't know what to do? Not that I think you are always in the same category every day. I think you, like me, find yourself wavering between the three. The only time someone is a mean girl all day, every day is in the movies. That's not real life.

I think we fall into one of three categories: the mean girl, the victim, or the bystander. Let's talk about each of these and how God intends us to behave, treat others, and somehow speak love, even when we are hurt.

The Mean Girl

If you are her . . .

You probably already know it. I did. Like I said, I don't think any of us are victims or mean girls all day, every day, but I had my days when I was a bully, mainly protecting my friends but sometimes also just because I was so insecure as a teenager that I wanted to do WHATEVER I could to feel better about me. So listen, there is grace for you. Really.

But you have to stop.

You are making fun of other girls because they aren't . . . what? Cool? Rich? Fun? Pretty?

Stop.

You are being sarcastic because you think it is funny? You are using biting words that are making others laugh at the price of one girl's feelings?

Stop.

The rest of your life you are going to be surrounded by people who are not as cool as you and people who are way cooler than you. You will get nowhere solid or fast by being unkind to those you think aren't as cool in hopes of being more like the ones you think are. I have this unique vantage point to your situation. I can see the adult women who used to be mean girls in my life who have chosen to stay that way. I'm not talking about the girls who sometimes were unkind; I'm talking about the ones who could wear the label. Want to know about them now as adults?

- They still have problems with girls and women.
- No one trusts them.
- They feel left out a lot.
- Other women can sense when they are acting like mean girls and so they slough them off.
- They still tear other people down because they are insecure.

I'm not hypothesizing; I'm telling you about people I still know. I'm just not using names, because when you use someone's name in a book you have to ask their permission and I don't want to inflict hurt. But trust me. The girls I am thinking of? They used to be on top of the pile, or so we all thought—and now, as adults, there is no pile. There are clumps of friends and there are some gals left standing alone.

The mean girls who became women? They are often alone.

Unless they chose a different way. Because you can quit and you can let God use your words to give life instead of death. You get that, right? That every time you pick on the girls at school or church (don't even GET me started on that), you are speaking death. You are tearing something apart. On the worst days, you're doing permanent damage.

But you can stop. You don't ever have to be her again. Your words can be life-giving, and you can recover and restore and try again. A Gilgal, if you will.

So how do you make the transition?

1. Ask God to forgive you.
2. Ask God to show you, in your heart, what the root of this thing is. Why are you insecure? Why do you need to be on the top of the food chain? What are you afraid of?
3. Talk to someone: a youth leader, your parents, a coach or teacher, someone who knows God and whom you trust. You need a mentor to help you with this.
4. Apologize to others if you need to.
5. Change. Your. Words.

Listen, it's not going to be easy. It's weird to acknowledge that you have used your words poorly and confess that to other people.

We've already talked about this verse, but I think it warrants being said again (and memorized).

JAMES 5:16

Confess your sins to each other and pray for each other so that you may be healed. The prayer of a righteous [person] is powerful and effective.

And listen, sister, I know what you are going through. Remember I had to write an entire CHAPTER apologizing for my words? Yeah, so I've been there.

Growing up, our church had discipleship groups for each grade and gender. My grade of girls was large, so we actually had three groups, I think. Our group—three leaders, twelve girls—met together, every Wednesday of the school year, from fourth grade until we graduated from high school. Yeah, long time. I remember being in the tenth grade and having a word revelation—I had been using my words wrong and I needed to apologize. So I wrote a letter.

We met in a Sunday school room. Everyone sat in small heavy wooden chairs around tables, and my hands shook as I held this letter I was afraid to read out loud. I breathed in, as my life-long friends stared at me and had no idea what was on that piece of paper.

It's been a lot of years but I can still feel that night. So yeah, I get it.

I read that letter and I apologized to these girls who had been around my words for eight solid years. They forgave me. I wish I still had that letter, but I remember that night saying to myself, "You could keep this and you may want to read it in the future, but I'd rather you throw it away. Just let it go."

(It's like Teen Annie knew that Author Annie might publish that letter someday. Smart girl.)

Every opportunity you take like that to apologize, to bring your meanness under the power of the Holy Spirit, your words shift and change. You'll be surprised to find that when you aren't the mean girl, you don't have to fight for friendships like you are in a battle. They just happen. In your head, you think that the best way to ensure you have friends is to be on the top of the pile. You're wrong, sister. Get down in the pile and make real, lasting friendships.

And remember this. Jesus Christ came so that you could have life, and HAVE IT MORE ABUNDANTLY (John 10:10). Sometimes the mean girl thinks that she has to decide who gets to stay and who had to go because she believes there are limited spots in the cool group. The illusion of limited resources is just that—an illusion. The whole food-chain friendship model? Get on the top or be eaten because there isn't enough space? That's not how Jesus works. He is all about abundance. There is enough. Enough of everything. So quit acting like there isn't.

Stop being the mean girl. Think before you speak. Speak life. It is time to change. Okay?

The Victim

If you are her . . .

I'm really sorry. It is a rare kind of pain to know another girl has it out for you and is seemingly trying to ruin your life. I am so sorry that she is (or they are) hurting you. It's never easy to pinpoint what makes you a target, and so not only are you suffering from words or actions, you are also questioning things about yourself. It's the worst.

Here's what I want you to know: It won't last forever. It

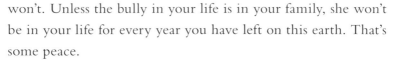

won't. Unless the bully in your life is in your family, she won't be in your life for every year you have left on this earth. That's some peace.

Remember this about the mean girl:

- She is hurting too, in a terribly deep way.
- She has no power over you.
- It's not your job to please her.

I wouldn't dream of assuming that I am an expert in how to help you or your situation, but here's what I know is true of you. You're probably great. You probably have lots of cool stories to tell and things that interest you. And I bet we'd be friends.

There was a girl on my bus in elementary school who always picked on me. Man, I could not figure out how to please her. For some reason, I thought that would fix things—if I made her happy. I believed that if I could somehow make her think I was cool, she would leave me alone. She never did.

One day, I read the coolest phrase in a book and decided the next afternoon I would say it to her on the bus and she would leave me alone.

So I mustered up all my guts and said, "Rocks and stones may break my bones but words will never hurt me."

She laughed. For two reasons that you and I can clearly see now.

1. I said the phrase wrong. (Doh!) It's "Sticks and stones . . ."
2. Words hurt. A lot. So that's the least true thing I could have said.

When we went to middle school, she was way more concerned about being cool to the eighth graders than she was about picking on a fellow sixth grader, so that was my real rescue from her.

I'm glad I said that to her on the bus that day, even if it didn't change her behavior all that much. That's only one time of two in my life that I went head to head with a bully. (And, just for your information, the second time was in seventh grade and was equally as awkward. Let's just say it included me putting my hands on a girl's shoulders and looking her in the eyes and saying, "You don't really want to punch me." So. I'm smoooooooth. Can you tell?)

On a bigger scale, let me tell you what the two of those girls mean to me now, as an adult: ABSOLUTELY NOTHING. The one from seventh grade sent me a friend request on Facebook and I laughed out loud. Now *she* wants to be *my* friend? Interesting. And no thanks.

You will survive this, friend. Those ugly words that are tossed at you like grenades and seem to explode and leave shrapnel in every corner of your being? You'll survive them.

Don't quit. Don't give up on life because of some mean girls. Here's what you should do:

- **Talk about it.** Tell an adult if you need to, or talk to your friends about it. Right now, everything feels dark and scary, but when you bring light into a place like that, all the pain seems to be less sharp. Try it. And if you feel like you are literally being psychologically tortured, you have got to tell someone you trust.
- **Believe Truth.** That's Truth with a capital T. There's a whole chapter about this coming up, so hang in there.

Believe what the Bible says about you. So even if some girl says you are ugly every day, believe the words that GOD has said about you—that you are flawless (see Song of Songs 4:7).

- **Find your people.** Part of the problem with mean girls is that in your heart you want them to think you are cool. I know; that was my problem too. But here's the thing: there are probably people right in front of you who you share interests or hobbies with. When you find your people—either in real life or maybe online—the mean girl loses power over your life.

- **Like what you want to like.** Be true to you. Most of all, first of all. After God's voice, the next voice that should have the most power in your life is your own. We're gonna talk more about this, but trust me when I say that you are free to be you.

- **Remember that her behavior doesn't determine YOUR behavior.** God has already taught us how to use our words. Just because someone is awful to you doesn't give you permission to be awful to other people—or to yourself.

- **Sometimes the best response is silence.** God always handles justice. And walking away from a situation, trusting that you don't have to inflict justice or defend yourself—sometimes that is the bravest thing you can do.

- **Sometimes the best response is speaking up for yourself.** Ask God to guide you, to fill you with wisdom and courage, and to know what to do in every situation.

If the majority of the mean girl junk in your life is going

on online, sign off. If that means you shut down your Facebook account or you get a new Instagram or whatever, do it. The thing about Internet bullies is that they can feel like they are SO VERY LOUD, but the truth is, just like with every other mean girl, they only have as much voice as you give them. If your computer is turned off and you are hanging with your family or friends, who cares what they say?

(Listen, I know. That's easier said than done. But just remember—YOU have the power to believe truth about yourself. If the only way your mind and heart can be healthy is to be off the Internet because people are awful, get off the Internet. We're gonna talk more about this in the next chapter . . . hang in there.)

Check out what Jesus said about enemies (and trust me, Jesus had enemies who said pretty awful stuff about Him).

MATTHEW 5:43–47

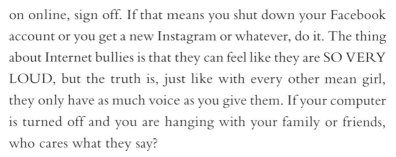

"You have heard that it was said, 'Love your neighbor and hate your enemy.' But I tell you: Love your enemies and pray for those who persecute you, that you may be [children] of your Father in heaven. He causes his sun to rise on the evil and the good, and sends rain on the righteous and the unrighteous. If you love those who love you, what reward will you get? Are not even the tax collectors doing that? And if you greet only your [own people], what are you doing more than others? Do not even pagans do that?"

Let your words still speak love, even to the enemies around you. Be different. Be you. Be love, like God is love. And be strong. You'll make it.

The Bystander

We've all been there. We've seen a girl or a few girls pick on another and we have either turned away or laughed along or felt weird but put our heads down. It's hard to know when to step in, isn't it? Because you don't want to become the target or put your nose in someone else's business, but you see the hurt going on and you know you could stop it.

Sadly, as adults, I think this is the most prevalent problem when it comes to mean girl stuff. Women do this weird passive-aggressive bully thing that, as you can imagine, makes me crazy. Even now, I watch as one of my friends is bullied in this way by her roommate. But what can I do? If I get involved, then what? I'm a hero and an enemy? I strain that relationship with one friend (because I'm friends with both of them) to protect another friend? I'll tell you what, it makes my forehead wrinkle and my eyebrows raise about twice a week, but I don't do anything.

Here's why. My friend who gets bullied? She asked me not to get involved. Oh, trust me, I offered. But she has asked me to stay out of it, so I do.

You may think I've become some sort of broken record, but the truth is that the solution is simple, from start to finish in this book. The truth stays the same.

Words are life. Pleasant words are sweet like honey.

You know what I do for my friend who gets bullied? Besides contort my face when she tells me stories of what is going on at home? I speak life over her. I tell her how great she is, I give her encouraging Bible verses, and I listen to her. My love for her can be a salve to heal the brokenness that the other woman causes.

So your gift to the girls in your life can be your words. To the bully? Yes, I think God may use you to speak life to her wounds that are causing her to act out like this. Matthew 5 also says, "Blessed are the peacemakers," and that can be you.

To the victim? Your kind words are a gift. They are medicine and they are a shield. You have no idea how one simple note or sentence can change the course of someone's heart path. You don't have to be confrontational or a fighter; you can be the one who heals. The one who gives life by sharing words that matter.

Yes, there are going to be times when you need to step in and protect someone, especially if you are in an authority role. Maybe you help with the elementary kids' church service or you coach Little League soccer. If so you should speak up for the girl who is being bullied to the point where she can't speak up for herself. But no matter your age, when you feel the moment come when you can rescue someone from the daggers of words pointed at their heart, do it.

The challenge here for me, and maybe you feel this too, is that I can accidentally lean toward bullying the bully, which is not right either. That's the other thing I have to be careful about in this situation with my two friends. Just because one girl is being a mean girl doesn't give me permission to hurt her with words or actions. On the other hand, you may lean toward staying quiet when you should speak up.

How do we know when to stop being the bystander and step in?

You pray for wisdom. You pray that God will make it very, very clear to you when your words are needed to defend someone else. And I'll be praying that for you too.

(And let's be clear. If someone is being bullied and you feel like they are in danger, emotionally or physically, you tell an adult. Like, yesterday. Be brave and do not fear. God is with you. Go to an adult and help rescue this mean girl victim.)

Note to Self: Don't Be Satan.

This is an epidemic in our society. "The Mean Girl" has been given too much power, too much popularity, and now it's like she lives in every neighborhood, goes to every school. And God have mercy, she's in every youth group.

I take her very seriously (can you tell?). I think we are a generation of women that could build each other into stronger godly women with the words we use, and instead women are often each other's worst enemies and words are the tools used to destroy.

Want me to get real for a minute? If you are using your words to destroy others, to hurt them, to kill their dreams, do you know who you sound like?

> **JOHN 10:10**
>
> The thief comes only to steal and kill and destroy; I have come that they may have life, and have it to the full.

Pardon my bluntness, but you sound like Satan.

We are the children of God, we are His people, we should sound like Him.

> **1 JOHN 4:19**
>
> We love because he first loved us.

If you could see me now, you would laugh. Today, I'm

standing up while I type, not like at a cool standup desk or something. My computer is on the dining room table and I just keep typing, then pacing the room, then heading back to the table to type again. I am so passionate about ending this—ending the Mean Girl Epidemic.

AND IT IS SO EASY. That's what makes me feel equally hopeful and furious.

Furious because the solution is so easy and hopeful because of you.

You are learning, and you already know, that words have power—that when you talk to God with your words, it changes things. That when you use your words well with others you can give them a gift of kindness. And that when you speak, every word is life or death. LIFE OR DEATH.

And now that you know, I think you are with me in this army against hateful words.

Can we just get rid of the mean girl? Will you quit being her? Will you quit bowing to her? Will you quit letting her exist?

I saw this sermon illustration one time that I thought was very wasteful, because as an eighth grader, I drank a lot of Coke.

Our pastor filled a pitcher halfway with Coke. Brown and bubbly and totally delicious. And then he started, as he talked, to pour water into the pitcher. As it filled, liquid poured out of it, a light brown mixture of the water and Coke. He continued to pour, and in time the Coke had all washed out and the only thing that glass pitcher held was clean water. The clean had cleared out the dirty.

Pour the words. The waterfall of words that give life. And let's wash away the darkness.

Your Words Matter

Memorize the Word

> Confess your sins to each other and pray for each other so that you may be healed. The prayer of a righteous [person] is powerful and effective.
>
> —JAMES 5:16

Read the Word

- Song of Songs 4:7
- Matthew 5:43–48
- John 10:10
- Use your concordance or BibleGateway.com to search these terms:
  - kindness
  - words

Journal Your Words

- Write the memory verse in your journal. As I said before, writing always helps me to actually memorize the Scripture quicker.
- Write about your experience with a mean girl.
- Ask God for wisdom in your situation.
- Make a list of girls you know are struggling with this—as the victim or even as the mean girl. Pray for them.

Use Your Words

- Send a note to two of your friends—one to a girl you think is the victim of bullying and another to a girl who sometimes is the mean girl. Encourage them. Tell them what you like about them. (This sounds scary—I know! But if we are going to end this thing, you're going to have to be brave, okay? Be brave.)

CHAPTER 8

Your Online Life

> Then I heard the voice of the Lord saying,
> "Whom shall I send? And who will go for us?"
> And I said, "Here am I. Send me!"
>
> —ISAIAH 6:8

If you like talking about the Internet, sister, you have come to the right place. I'm a big fan of the World Wide Web.

You've Got Mail is still my favorite movie. Maybe it's because the main character owns a tiny, beautiful bookstore, or maybe it's the overuse of twinkly lights, daffodils, tissues, and knee-length skirts, but if that movie comes on the television, I can hardly walk away.

Back when it first came out, the idea that you would MEET A PERSON ON THE INTERNET was so foreign and creepy that it really forged new territory. Back then, chat rooms were only for perverts, and connecting with a stranger on the other side of the computer was guaranteeing that you were IMing with a fifty-year-old dude who still lived in his mom's basement.

Ew.

Today? My seventeen-year-old friend Anne tells me how she has a new best friend in London who sent her a Christmas present, and how did they meet? Thanks to the Steam Powered Giraffe fandom Tumblr.

I know. Those five words don't make any sense to most of us because you actually cannot steam power a giraffe, and a fandom is not a real thing, and you forgot the "e" in tumblr. Trust me, if you said "Steam Powered Giraffe fandom Tumblr" to my grandmother, she would think you had fallen down at the zoo in July.

But it is. It is a real thing. And the band doesn't do much except make music and, though I don't exactly understand why, they dress like metallic robots from 1922.

What the fans do is the amazing part. They become friends with each other. They click here and there, and within minutes they are connected with other fans who love Steam Powered Giraffe. The band doesn't do anything to cultivate friendships within their fan base. They just create music and the fans connect with each other.

Last week, Anne's mom and I were texting about a French dip recipe (Want it? It's in the appendix) when suddenly her text tone changed (know what I mean?). She told me Anne had just gotten a phone call from another online friend, this one across the US from her. That friend's dad had just been killed in a car wreck, and who did she call? Anne.

No, they didn't grow up together. No, they can't drive to each other's houses. But their friendship and connection, while building it around this weird band that makes music my thirty-three-year-old ears do not prefer, was much deeper and more profound than I would have guessed online friendships could become.

That's where things are going, isn't it?

A few months ago I drove to Birmingham for a speaking engagement. When I had a break in the afternoon, I pointed my car through the backwoods of some part of Alabama I did not know and drove to LoraLynn's house. She and her husband have seven children under seven (it involved adoption and twins in case the math was getting you down), and when I arrived we sat on the couch and talked about life, and I cried about heartache while the kids wove in and out of the room. I told her the real stuff, and she told me the same.

LoraLynn and I met on the Internet.

I recently wrote a blog post about one of my college roommates, Eve. We had a great house of six girls who lived together for a few years. We left our Christmas tree up far into the spring season and ate too much ranch-flavored Suddenly Salad pasta salad. Three of us went to Dairy Queen one day in the summer, and between us we had $2.50 in quarters and three flip-flops. THREE. I hope you are picturing the classy display that we were. I really loved that house of girls. But here we are, a bunch of years later, and I don't even have all of their phone numbers or mailing addresses anymore. But we're all friends on Facebook, and when I wrote the post about Eve, I posted it to her wall so she would see it. Within a few hours, we had a whole conversation going on around that one post about the year we put on turtlenecks and went to the Walmart photo studio to make Christmas cards. (We were awesome roommates.)

The Internet keeps us together, and I'm grateful. On its

best-behaved days, I've seen the Internet make friends, grow friendships, and be the string that ties together old friendships that might otherwise break apart.

But the Internet doesn't always behave.

Mean Internet

Today I googled "cyberbullying" because I wanted to read a story or two about the ugly side of the Internet. We all know it is out there—rampant pornography, tutorials on violence and hate, celebrated racism. I know that bullying happens online as much as, if not more than, it happens at school or church or wherever. But I wanted some stats and some facts.

Every culture has its villains and every society has evil. That is true of the modern-day Wild, Wild West that is the World Wide Web. You know, there is NOWHERE ELSE IN THE WORLD where this many people can get together without any laws or police. I can't go to a Georgia Bulldogs game with 92,746 of my closest friends without passing by a ticket taker, walking by K9 cops with their smart-nosed dogs, and pushing past fences. That's not true of the Internet. As of January 2013, Facebook alone had one billion users, YouTube had 800 million, and there were 150 million Tumblr accounts. And not one Internet police officer.

When I got to Google and started snooping around about cyberbullying, to be honest? It ruined my day. The stories of how students treat each other online could make you literally throw up. One article listed the names of students who had committed suicide related to cyberbullying. Each name was hyperlinked, so you could click on it and read their news stories. And while that is just a paragraph of names, each of those names has a mom and a dad. Probably brothers and sisters have walked by an empty bedroom that used to belong to one of those kids. Teenagers have lost their friends.

According to mashable.com, from 1985–2007, Internet and technology grew rapidly (duh), but so did teen suicides. In fact, the Center for Disease Control found that suicide rates in girls fifteen to nineteen rose 32 percent and rose 76 percent in girls ten to fourteen.[1]

You can say that is a coincidence, but I don't think it is.

It's heartbreaking. And it is too much for my brain to understand.

In 2012, CovenantEyes.com released stats related to cyber-bullying. According to their research, "41% of older girls (fifteen to seventeen) report being bullied [online], more than any other gender or age group."[2] That means of your small group at church of twelve girls, five of them could be being bullied online right now. RIGHT NOW.

Do you know which five?

Are you one of them?

Are you the bully?

I also discovered on that same site that 88 percent of social media-using teens say they have seen someone be mean or cruel

---

1   "Dramatic Increase in Teen Suicide," WebMD Health News, September 6, 2007, www.webmd.com/mental-health/news/20070906/dramatic-increase-in-teen-suicide

2   "Bullying Statistics: Fast Facts About Cyberbullying," Covenant Eyes Breaking Free Blog, January 17, 2012, www.covenanteyes.com/2012/01/17/bullying-statistics-fast-facts-about-cyberbullying/

to another person on a social network site, and 12 percent of these say they witness this kind of behavior "frequently."

Frequently?

We've talked a lot about the mean girl and her words in the last chapter, so I won't linger here. But you know what I know—the Internet can be a heartbreaking place.

So I read tons online about cyberbullying, and at the bottom of one of the articles, it said, "Internet, cellphone, and social media use will all continue to grow among teens. But if more and more people speak up, bullying doesn't have to."

Amen.

We can talk all day long about all the awful corners of the Internet, but instead, I want to talk about how we can become the stronger voice online.

Get Loud

Here's something true: you are part of the loudest generation that has ever existed. Never before has a group of people been given the voice and access that we all have now.

My social sciences teacher did a really cool experiment with our class in the ninth grade. (I couldn't exactly remember how this story went, so—thank you, technology—I Facebooked my teacher from twenty years ago and he remembered. Well done, Mr. Lynch!)

Our class made up a word. It was a word that no one had ever seen or used before—PPM. He asked us, for one week, to write those letters everywhere: put it on our lockers, write it in notes, pretty much paper our school in PPM. There were only about fifteen of us in this particular class, but after a week of writing

PPM around the school, lots of other kids started using it too. We would get together in class and laugh hysterically—how in the WORLD did these hundreds of high schoolers decide to graffiti our letters all over the place and why? It didn't make sense, but it worked.

We had created a fad, a buzzword, something that caught on.

I was shocked. Here we were, a freshman social sciences class with fifteen people who had just influenced our entire school of hundreds of students to use some crazy letter pattern we created.

This is true of me and this is true of you; we love being told what is cool. That's why fashion magazines sell and that's what buzzfeed.com excels at—showing you what other people think is cool so that you can know what is cool.

Or perceived as cool, at least.

And here you are, with all the tools you could ever need (assuming you are on the Internet in some capacity) to help people decide what is cool and what is worth talking about.[3]

Those of you on the Internet, you are loud, my friends. You are. If all of you decided on one day to write on Facebook, "Don't wear red anymore," our favorite clothing companies would quit making red clothing. Plain and simple. You are able to constantly express your opinions and emotions and people are listening.

Louie Giglio and the Passion Movement have created an anti-slavery organization called The END IT Movement. All they ask of students like you? Awareness. They just want you

---

3   And even if your parents won't let you have a Facebook page yet, or you don't have a smartphone so you can't do Twitter and Instagram, no biggie. The Internet isn't going anywhere, and you'll have your chance. But right now you can think and pray about what you want your online life to look like.

to talk about it, tweet about it, like them on Facebook—those kinds of things. Because they know what we know: when you talk about something online, it changes things.

It's time to get loud. It's time to use your social media presence to share truth with people. When we share who God is and how He loves, we can make a difference in the world.

MATTHEW 5:14–16

You are the light of the world. A city on a hill cannot be hidden. Neither do people light a lamp and put it under a bowl. Instead they put it on its stand, and it gives light to everyone in the house. In the same way, let your light shine before [others], that they may see your good deeds and glorify your Father in heaven.

I wonder if Jesus was thinking about the Internet when He said this to the crowds gathered to hear Him speak some two thousand years ago. Sure, they didn't have a clue what was coming in the future, but He did.

My heart has known the song "This Little Light of Mine" for my whole life, but I don't know that it has ever impacted me, truly, the way it does when I think about our ability to affect the world online.

Before I was a book writer, I was a blogger. (I still am a blogger: anniefdowns.com/blog.) When I first started, I knew about five people with a blog. They all went to my church. I didn't realize that there was a whole other world on the Internet where bloggers existed and knew each other and kept up with each other's lives.

I just started writing for those five. For my friends. I began to tell stories of my days in the classroom as an elementary teacher, my church experiences, concerts, sports events, and the ridiculous things that seem to happen to me a lot. And before I knew it, there were strangers reading what I wrote. I would have ten readers one day and then fifteen the next. Within a few months there were one hundred people reading about my life Monday through Friday. And then it just kept growing.

My blog audience has watched, firsthand, as God moved me from Marietta, Georgia, to Nashville, Tennessee, to Edinburgh, Scotland, and back to Nashville. They've seen me quit teaching school, pursue writing, and then actually become a writer. They have read about my best and my worst days—at least the events that were appropriate and important to share.

My light, while sometimes foggy and often dim and flawed, has shown over the city of people who come to my website every day. And God is glorified, even in my mistakes. They don't have to really know me, and I don't have to see them, for them to experience God through my life.

I don't care the medium. Facebook. Twitter. Blog. Instagram. Tumblr. Pinterest. You have so many chances to share light, to share God, to make Him known to the people who listen to your voice.

My friend Anne, the one who loves Steam Powered Giraffe? She texted me last week and said, "I'm trying to use my Tumblr as a way to positively influence my followers through God."

And that's shining your light into a dark place.

What Does That Look Like?

So how do you do it? Here are some stories from people I know:

Angelica is a seventeen-year-old, redheaded beauty from Scotland. You know the movie *Brave*? Yeah, that's what she looks like, but she's braver and cuter. Almost every day, Angelica uses Facebook to post a different recipe she is making, and they all look delicious. She also talks about Jesus. She shares verses, song lyrics, or just her thoughts on who God is and what He is doing in her life. It's not obnoxious, and she doesn't judge people. She just shares about her life and how God is a big part of her life. It's really beautiful.

My friend Matt uses Instagram to take pictures of Bible verses, then he underlines important parts of the verse, things that stand out to him. His website is called Versify:Life. So cool.

Jennie Allen, one of my favorite authors and a dear friend, uses her blog to tell people about the struggles she and her friends and family are going through and how God has shown up for them every step of the pain.

Kendall, one of the beauties in my small group, has a board on Pinterest she uses to pin Bible verses and other inspirational things that remind her of God.

Carlos is a worship leader who uses Twitter to challenge Christians to live more openly and honestly.

Christy works for Dave Ramsey, and at the bottom of each of her emails is a verse reminding us to trust God with our finances. (Yes and amen.)

These friends? They are loud for God with their Internet. They aren't necessarily being preachy, but they aren't hiding their light either.

In the end, your words on the Internet are as important as the words that come out of your mouth.

And while the mouth can speak love, the hands type it.

People can be changed by that. I try to blog three to four times a week, and I can't tell you how many emails I get from people saying that God spoke to them through something I wrote. But that's not why I do it—I'm not tooting my own horn here, friend, I'm just saying that I write on my computer, push publish, then walk away and live my life, and God uses the stories to tell other people about Him.

Why? Because God loves to speak love to others THROUGH US. He loves for us to be involved with His redemption plan for this world.

I am reminded of a verse in Isaiah.

ISAIAH 6:8

Then I heard the voice of the Lord saying, "Whom shall I send? And who will go for us?"

And I said, "Here am I. Send me!"

And that is my prayer for my life on the Internet.

As I write today, and think about you, I'm in my favorite coffee shop again, Portland Brew, and tears are just puddling in my eyes as I read these verses and think about the ways that the people in your life, the hurt ones, the sad ones, the broken ones, can hear hope from you.

ISAIAH 40:9–11 (**THE MESSAGE**)

Climb a high mountain, Zion.

You're the preacher of good news.

Raise your voice.

> Make it good and loud, Jerusalem.
>
> You're the preacher of good news.
>
> Speak loud and clear. Don't be timid!
>
> Tell the cities of Judah,
>
> "Look! Your God!"
>
> Look at him! God, the Master, comes in power,
>
> ready to go into action.
>
> He is going to pay back his enemies
>
> and reward those who have loved him.

Does that make you want to stand up on your chair and cheer and yell and tell the world?! Or is that just me?

You are the preacher of good news.

Raise. Your. Voice.

Remember that song I told you about when we talked about worship? "All the Poor and Powerless" by All Sons & Daughters says:

> Shout it. Go on and scream it from the mountains.
> Go on and tell it to the masses.
> That He is God.

That was my theme last year. I prayed it, I sang it, I posted it on Instagram, I wrote it on the cover of my journal.

You don't have to climb a mountain. But you can tell it to

the masses—your Facebook friends, the ones who repost your pics on Instagram or follow you on Twitter or connect with you on whatever new site you're using. You can start something—a website, a hashtag, an online community, a blog, a Tumblr—to create a place on the Internet where people go to find hope and joy and learn more about God.

And that's what I pray for you. I pray that you are the kind of girl who, all over the Internet, doesn't use your words to tear down other people online. Cyberbullying is horrible and wrong and, as you've heard me say before, if you are using your words to kill, steal, or destroy someone, you don't sound like God. You sound like the enemy.

And remember—the only reason that Satan is attacking people online is because HE KNOWS THE POWER that exists there for good. He knows. He is always out to destroy the things that God can use for His glory. There is battle online, and you are involved every day; a battle between good and evil, between hope and hopelessness, between light and dark.

I pray you are the light. I pray that you are inspired to see your Internet life for what it is—a large stage, with all eyes on you, the audience waiting to hear about your life and your God and the hope that they can have.

Remember this truth: you are always speaking life or death. Every time. And what if we all decided to be a tidal wave of words of life that wash over the Internet?

Things would change, my friend. They would change.

You are the preacher of good news.

Raise. Your. VOICE.

Your Words Matter

Memorize the Word

> Then I heard the voice of the Lord saying, "Whom shall I send? And who will go for us?"
>
> And I said, "Here am I. Send me!"
>
> —ISAIAH 6:8

Read the Word

- Luke 6:45
- Matthew 5
  - Jesus stood in front of a crowd and spoke truth over and over. Read this chapter and underline the verses that stand out to you.
- Isaiah 40
  - Wow, wow, wow. This whole chapter is full of beautiful words about who God is and how He rescues us.

Journal Your Words

- Write the memory verse in your journal.
- Have you seen online bullying? Have you been bullied online? Write about that. (And listen, sister, if it is really bad, you need to tell someone. Getting off the Internet is one solution, but if that isn't stopping the bullying, adults need to know. Okay? Okay.)
- If you don't use the Internet on a regular basis, what are some ways you can pray for other people who are online?

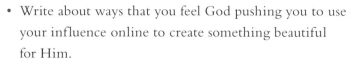

- Write about ways that you feel God pushing you to use your influence online to create something beautiful for Him.
- How do you want to use the Internet to spread the gospel? To talk about God?

Use Your Words

- Find your favorite Bible verse—maybe one of our memory verses?—and tweet it out. Use the hashtag #SpeakLove so that we can all see the Scriptures that are encouraging you.
- Build a board on Pinterest and label it Speak Love. Collect visual images and words that speak to you and remind you of God and how He feels about you.
- Are we already connected online? If not, find my Facebook page (Facebook.com/anniefdowns) and post on my wall about what God is showing you as you read.
- Blog about the first time you remember God answering your prayers.
- Follow the hashtag #SpeakLove and see what other people are saying and how they are encouraging each other.

CHAPTER 9

Celebrities Big and Small

> Seek justice, encourage the oppressed. Defend
> the cause of the fatherless, plead the case of the
> widow.
>
> —ISAIAH 1:17

We've spent significant time discussing how you use your words with the people you know. But what about the few billion people on the planet you don't know? Can you use your words to make a difference in their lives too?

I'm gonna say yes. I think you can. I think the people who are most affected by your voice are the ones in your life every day, but there is real power in speaking to and for the people on the planet you've never met.

For my job, I write books for people I don't know. I mean, that's technically the truth, but if I'm being honest, I kinda feel like you are my friend. In my heart, I feel like we know each other. Maybe that makes me a loony bird. (Probably.) But every day that I write, I start by praying, begging God to give me the right words for you and the right words for this book. And as we talked about in the last chapter, I blog a few times a week for that group of friends as well.

Also, every Tuesday night around 6:30, twelve Belmont University girls show up at my house and we eat dinner and talk about the Bible and pray together. Most Thursday nights, I eat barbeque with some baseball players from Vanderbilt who have become like my little brothers.

I use words all day long, but they are different from one group to the other. The things I say to my girls, the things I say to my baseball boys, and the things I say to you are all different. All those words are important, though the audiences are different and their needs are unique.

If you ask me to list the places where I use my words to help others know God better, those are the four groups (besides my friends and family): my small group, my Vandybros, my blog friends, and you, my readers.

Half of them I actually know, and the other half I just feel like I know. Both audiences are important. That's why I'm telling all this to you—there are many people in your life who should hear your words of life and love, but there are also people outside your circle whom you can speak to and speak for, changing lives in ways you may never know.

Honestly, I think that some of the most powerful ways to use your words can be to people you may never meet. There are three big categories of people to whom your words matter: celebrities, people without a voice of their own, and people who receive the art you make.

Celebrities

Many moons ago, NSYNC was my favorite boy band. Let's be serious, they still are, even though they are no longer a band. ("Band" might be a generous term since none of them played instruments. Let's go with "group.") Two of my best friends from college were big fans as well, but luckily we all had a different favorite member.

We were super fans. I'm not afraid to say it.

We paid good money for eighteenth-row seats at their stadium concert in Atlanta. We watched and recorded every television appearance. We bought magazines. We were borderline creepy.

The key word there being "borderline." Okay? I promise we weren't stalkers. (Are you still my friend? I hope so.)

This was in the days before social media was a thing, so we had no direct access to them except via mail. Like, snail mail. Like, write in a birthday card and mail it to the address on the back of the CD pamphlet and hope that your favorite member of NSYNC actually reads the card.

Ahem. Something like that.

But today is very different. You can easily find all your favorite celebrities with little trouble. And you can talk RIGHT TO THEM in an instant. Thanks to social media, the days of "fan mail" are quickly disappearing. Instead you can like your favorite singer on Facebook and follow him on Twitter and tweet him, and he may actually see your tweet.

It's weird, actually. It's weird that we have direct access to these people who are famous. And we expect them to listen to us and respond, don't we? Never before have celebrities appeared this available.

For girls like us, the ones who want to use our words to speak life and love to those around us, this is great news. If we can avoid being creepy stalker girls and instead use our power to bring life, we could have a bigger influence than we'll ever know.

(To make our lives easier, I'm going to talk about a celebrity we're simply going to call "That Famous Guy." Now, in your mind, picture who That Famous Guy is for you. And if your favorite celebrity is a girl, or a group, or even a computer-generated character in a commercial, just trade out the name and pronouns. Got it? Okay, continue on.)

Here are some things about talking to celebrities:

1. You don't love That Famous Guy.

Sorry to break your heart, but you don't actually know him. You know his public persona and the things he is willing to share. But love comes from living day in and day out with people, dealing with their good and their bad, and being invested in their lives while they are invested in yours. THAT is love.

I get it. You may feel like what you are feeling is love. I've been there. And while you may think That Famous Guy is super awesome and an incredible musician or whatever, you don't really know him.

And when you talk to celebrities, remember you don't actually know them, so you can't love them. So tweeting, "I LOVE YOU, FAMOUS GUY!" is not a true way to speak life.

2. That Famous Guy has feelings too.

After the Grammys in 2013, people were seriously unkind to Taylor Swift because they thought she was making fun of Harry

Styles. All over the Internet, young women tweeted and tumbled death threats to Taylor because she spoke in a British accent during her performance of a break-up song.

Seriously?

There are two problems here. First problem goes back to #1—all those girls felt like they really loved and cared for Harry Styles, one of the singers in One Direction and former flame of TSwift. Listen, I think he is adorable, but most people, dare I say EVERY person, who tweeted something horrible to Taylor probably didn't actually know either of them.

Celebrities are real people, just like you and me, and they have feelings.

I think it's important to know that no matter how many followers or friends a celebrity has online, they are still human. That Famous Guy is still a real person, and he can see what people say to him and about him online.

Some of my more famous friends here in Nashville can have some terrible things written about them online, from people and from tabloids. I've sat there and watched them read the ugly things firsthand, and it is painful.

So if you are going to be a voice to your favorite celebrities, be kind with your words. You are talking to a human.

3. You should speak life to That Famous Guy.

So instead of being a voice that hurts, why not be a voice that speaks life? I think we all underestimate the pressures and pains that go along with all the good of being super famous (or even mildly famous). Girls like us? We should be the ones encouraging and speaking the words that will bless, not curse.

PROVERBS 21:1

The king's heart is in the hand of the Lord; he directs it like a watercourse wherever he pleases.

Remember that God holds every heart in His hands, and He could use you as a tool to speak life and direction in the heart of someone who may not know any other Christians.

I am definitely *not* saying that it is ungodly to talk to celebrities via social media, or send a letter, or meet them in person, or whatever. I'm just saying that we should use our words to bless with balance.

Telling That Famous Guy that God loves him? Totally.

Tweeting That Famous Guy and telling him that you love his work? Do it.

Thanking That Famous Guy for his last Facebook post that really meant something to you? Yes.

Responding to a Facebook post with a Bible verse of encouragement? Game on.

I've watched my famous friends be really blessed and moved by kind notes, meaningful tweets, or emails. Truly. Sometimes God uses fans like us to speak life. So go for it! Remember all the haters who wrote to Taylor Swift? Be a different voice.

4. Lower your expectations.

Last but not least, remember that you aren't using your words for famous people because you are expecting something back. That's not why we show love to anyone. It's selfish to speak life in order to get words back.

So when you go forth and speak life and love, do it because

it is the right way to bless someone whose art you have grown to love and appreciate.

The Voiceless

There is a social enterprise here in Nashville called Thistle Farms. As a part of Magdalene, a residential program for women who have survived prostitution, trafficking, addiction, and life on the streets, the graduates are then employed by Thistle Farms to make body care products like lotions, candles, and soaps.

And the products smell like perfection.

A few weeks ago, my friend Matt Wertz planned a Thistle Farms party at his house. I pictured it being like one of those jewelry parties, where there are snacks and some sort of fizzy punch. Around the room would be tables covered in jewelry, and you'd need to buy at least one thing because your friend who invited you would be trying to earn a free diamond bracelet or something.

But Wertz's plan was different. The women from Thistle Farms were coming over to his house to tell us their stories, sharing with us where they had been, where they were going, and what God had done in their hearts in the process.

It wasn't just about buying their products; it was about hearing their voices.

Wertz used his voice to make a way for restored women to share their stories.

Incredible idea, I think.

I don't care how old or how young you are; you have a voice. And one of the very best ways you can use the voice you've been given is to speak up for those who do not have a voice or do not have the ability to use their voices.

Over and over again, the Bible tells us to do just that.

ISAIAH 1:17

Seek justice, encourage the oppressed. Defend the cause of the fatherless, plead the case of the widow.

JAMES 1:27

Religion that God our Father accepts as pure and faultless is this: to look after orphans and widows in their distress and to keep oneself from being polluted by the world.

And there are plenty more places in the Bible where we are told to step in and help those who are in need. If you've been in church for a while, then you probably have had offers to go on mission trips or serve at your local soup kitchen. I believe all that is very valuable and important; using our hands and our time to serve others is a big part of our faith.

But every day, you have the chance to use your words to speak on behalf of those who don't have a voice for themselves.

My friend Susan Norris wrote a novel called *Rescuing Hope*, which follows the story of a young teen girl as she is captured by a life of sex slavery in Atlanta, Georgia. Susan, as an author and speaker, educates people on behalf of girls who are trapped in that lifestyle. While she may not be out on the streets pulling the girls to safety in the middle of the night, her words are opening the eyes of many readers and motivating them to do something—whether that is donating time or money or giving a voice to this cause.

There are many ways that you can use your voice to affect people in need in your area or your country. Here are a few ideas:

- Write an article for your school paper about the homeless shelter in your area and how people can volunteer there.
- Use your social media outlets (Facebook, Twitter, etc.) to talk about nonprofit organizations in your town, sharing their needs or events.
- Like the Facebook pages of organizations that you care about and share their status updates.

My friend Aimee homeschools her kids. A few weeks ago, the homeless shelter in our hometown put on Facebook that it was running low on food. So she gave each of her kids a small budget, and for their math lesson they went to the grocery store to buy supplies for the homeless shelter. Then she posted the pictures of their day out on Facebook so that all our friends could see the idea. And others did it too!

It didn't take a lot of work on her part, but she was able to help the shelter as well as encourage others to do the same, just by sharing her story.

My friend Jeremy Cowart is a professional photographer. He created a nonprofit organization called Help-Portrait that provides professional portraits for people in need around the world. When he came up with this idea, all he did was make a video saying, "Hey, photographers, why not get together on the first Saturday in December and head to your local shelter and take pictures of those in need this Christmas?" It wasn't an expensive idea, and it wasn't complicated: Just take pictures and give the photos away for free.

Jeremy used his voice to share an idea that helped other people, and since December 2009 there have been over 382,000 portraits taken by tens of thousands of photographers around the world. Literally—I'm talking in over sixty countries. Crazy.

Do you dig that or what?

One guy. One idea. One video. And in less than a few years, over a quarter of a million pictures were snapped because of this one idea.

That is using your voice, huh?

You can do the same. Have an idea? Want your friends to get together and raise money for a cancer patient? Or get your school to send letters to kids your age in a different city or country? Or create a Facebook page to highlight all the nonprofits in your town that are doing good work? Go for it!

Figure out what you care about—caring for orphans, serving the homeless, stopping sex trafficking, or other things you feel called to do—and use your voice to tell other people about it.

Not only does it matter for things locally, but your voice can make a huge difference in speaking into needs globally.

Speaking of Jeremy Cowart, he and I wrote a book together called *What's Your Mark?* In the book, Jeremy photographed twenty people who are making a mark on the world, and I got to interview them. It was one of the greatest honors of my life. After almost every interview, I would hang up the phone and sit and cry, thinking of all the things these people were doing for the world. Whether it was the teen girl who created a 5K race to raise money for a high school in Africa or the famous television producer using his ability to tell stories to make a miniseries about the Bible, they were all using their voices to influence others and change the world.

There are so many nonprofit organizations that are doing good work. I think of International Justice Mission that provides help and hope for the oppressed, or Blood:Water Mission that works to provide clean water and health care to those who can't afford it. (Want to know more? Check the appendix for information on these and more nonprofits that could use your voice to help raise awareness.)

I use my voice to raise awareness and speak on behalf of the Mocha Club. Mocha Club does relief work all over Africa, but I am personally connected to and invested in their education work. As a former elementary school teacher, it is important to me that kids around the world get the opportunity to learn to read and write and experience all the things that a proper education offers. I donate a little money every month—only nine dollars—that is put toward education projects. I've been to South Africa with Mocha Club and seen firsthand the good works they are doing there to educate children and adults and give them the chance to compete in a world market. It's incredible.

I think my favorite project that I help support through Mocha Club is New Dawn High School in Kenya. Teenagers from the largest slum in Nairobi are now able to attend school, use computers, do science experiments, and read new books thanks to what the Mocha Club has done. When I saw the pictures of the first graduating class, I cried (shocking no one). It was just beautiful to see the faces of those smiling seniors, realizing that while many of their friends will never leave the slums because they have no way out, these teens now have an education and a future. Because of the Mocha Club.

Nine dollars a month isn't much. It's like two soy chais a month, or two mochas a month. (Eh—get it? Mocha Club? Genius.) No biggie. So obviously, I'm not making the hugest financial difference to this organization. But you know what matters more? My voice. Raising awareness of all the good things that Mocha Club is doing across the continent of Africa is just as important, if not more important, than my little nine bucks a month.[1]

There are many nonprofits looking for people just like you to use their voices to make an impact. It doesn't take much. A blog post here. A conversation there. A Facebook status once in a while.

And of course, if you want, you can go on mission trips and use your words to preach the Gospel of Jesus Christ to people who need to know Him. You don't have to stay home and use your words—go to the places where people haven't heard of Jesus and tell them! I love short-term and long-term missions; being face to face with people who are from a different culture and need Jesus will change you, and change them, forever.

Your Art

A few weekends ago, I was speaking at a retreat, and on Saturday afternoon we did a short question and answer session. I absolutely love this part of retreats because you guys ask me some of the funniest questions ever.

---

1   By the way, if you want to join my team and donate to education projects in Africa, like New Dawn High School in Kenya, head to www.themochaclub.org/annie.

I think there is an assumption that because I live in Nashville I know every famous country music artist in the world. So I usually have to skip over about one-third of the questions because they are things like, "Does Taylor Swift eat Doritos Loco Tacos from Taco Bell?" (And how am I supposed to know THAT?) But most of the questions are sweet and deep and really express what is going on in the hearts of the girls in the crowd.

My favorite one from this recent retreat was, "I want to be a singer and a songwriter. What do you recommend I do to get to do that?"

It reminded me of a Facebook message I got a few months ago where a student told me that she felt God was calling her to be a speaker, so she wanted to do that when she grows up.

I asked them both the same thing.

Why wait?

Why are you waiting until you grow up to make art that changes the world? You want to make music? Learn an instrument, write some songs, record yourself, and post it on YouTube. Or ask your youth pastor if you can help lead worship on a retreat. Write poems and fill notebooks with stories and share them with your friends. Want to be a speaker and tell people about Jesus? Volunteer to teach third-grade Sunday school at your church or ask your Fellowship of Christian Athletes leader if you can speak at a meeting one week.

A lot of the students in our college ministry at my church are involved with Young Life. I love Young Life and what it does for students. And each week, the director allows one of the college students to share what God is teaching him or her.

I listened yesterday as one of the students shared with me what he felt God has laid on his heart to teach the other students.

I tried AS HARD AS I COULD not to cry (because, seriously, my tears can get so annoying to me), but hearing how he had read Scripture, applied it to his life, and was ready to teach that lesson to others really moved me.

Is he a professional speaker or teacher? Nope. But what God showed him changed me. It also impacted the students to whom he was speaking when he stood in front of them that night.

You are going to put words out to the world—whether that's a book or a Facebook post or a note in a yearbook. And for many of you, you will influence people whom you will never meet with the words you write, sing, draw, or say.

I want you to remember that when we talk about using our voices for other people, it isn't just about the less fortunate (though it is! And what a powerful thing!). You also need to think about the people who receive your art—the ones who will read your words or your social media pages, hang your art in their home, or play your songs on their phone.

My friend Jenni Catron leads a women's group at my church, and she often shares these verses with us:

GALATIANS 6:4-5 (THE MESSAGE)

Make a careful exploration of who you are and the work you have been given, and then sink yourself into that. Don't be impressed with yourself. Don't compare yourself with others. Each of you must take responsibility for doing the creative best you can with your own life.

It doesn't say to sink yourself in the creative best once you are an adult. Start now! If we want to talk about celebrities big and small, remember that to someone, that's you. Whether it is a crowd of tens of thousands listening to Hillary Scott from Lady Antebellum or crowds of tens in your Bible study listening to you, someone is listening. Someone cares what you think. Someone is making decisions, at least in part, based on what you think and say.

It could be your little sister or your entire school.

As I told you at the beginning of this chapter, I have a lot of different groups that hear different things from me. But trust me, every day I think about you. I think about the girls who are reading my books or my Facebook page or my blog looking for advice or help or direction. I may never know your face or phone number, but I think about you and, when I'm writing, all I can pray is that God gives me all the right words for you. I take my art seriously. I take God's ability to use it for His glory even more seriously. You do your work one time—compose the song, illustrate the Bible verse into a piece of art, write the poem—but then the ones who receive your art get it over and over again.

I've had the singer/songwriter husband/wife duo Elenowen on repeat for days. (Want to know what else I've listened to while writing this book? Check the appendix and get ready for some of the best music you've probably never heard.) Every time I hear a song by Elenowen, they do not have to create it all over again. They made it once, I enjoy it hundreds of times.

(Literally. Hundreds. I have an issue with the replay button. I like to push it.)

Remember that when you make your art. Work hard to honor God with your words and your creations because once you make them, they're out there, ready to glorify God in the lives of many people.

You will never know. I will never know. We will never know

the full impact of our words or our lives. So we just live, wide open, encouraging others, sharing whenever we can, speaking up for those who don't have a voice, and creating art that points to who God is and how He loves.

ISAIAH 52:7 (**THE MESSAGE**)

How beautiful on the mountains are the feet of the messenger bringing good news,

Breaking the news that all's well, proclaiming good times, announcing salvation, telling Zion, "Your God reigns!"

It's not just the feet that are beautiful, it's the voice. Proclaiming. Telling everyone within earshot that God reigns.

Shout it.

Go on and scream it from the mountains.

Go on and tell it to the masses.

That He is God.

Your Words Matter

Memorize the Word

Seek justice, encourage the oppressed. Defend the cause of the fatherless, plead the case of the widow.

—ISAIAH 1:17

(Want a cool challenge? Memorize Galatians 6:4–5 in *The Message* version. That's what I'm working on right now.)

Read the Word

- Proverbs 21:1
- James 1:27
- Galatians 6:4–5
- Isaiah 52:7
- Use BibleGateway.com or your concordance to look for other verses using these key words:
  - orphans
  - widows
  - help
  - fatherless
  - create

Journal Your Words

- Write the memory verse in your journal, especially if you are going for that big boy in Galatians. ☺
- Make a list (SHORT list) of the celebrities who you really feel like God has placed on your heart to encourage. Pray for them for a few days before you say anything. Ask God to put on your heart the exact right words for them.
- Journal your answers to the following questions:
  - Why do we love celebrities so much?
  - How can you see God using your art to impact the world?
  - What nonprofit organizations in your town are interesting to you?
  - What nonprofit organizations that do work globally would you like to use your voice to help raise awareness?

⦿ If you could go anywhere in the world to share the gospel, where would you go? How long would you stay?

Use Your Words

- Create something! Pick your favorite verse, grab a pack of markers and a few sheets of paper, and use fun lettering to make a piece of art using your favorite verse.
- Use social media outlets (Instagram, Twitter, etc.) to say something encouraging to the celebrities you really like. Use the hashtag #SpeakLove
- Get involved with a local nonprofit organization so that you can use your words on behalf of those who can't speak for themselves.
- Write a blog post or post on one of your social networks about how you want to use your voice to help others.

CHAPTER 10

Talking about God

In your hearts set apart Christ as Lord. Always be prepared to give an answer to everyone who asks you to give the reason for the hope that you have. But do this with gentleness and respect.

—1 PETER 3:15

When I was working on *What's Your Mark?* with Jeremy Cowart, I was so nervous before some of those interviews that I can't even put it in words for you. I knew I would be getting on the phone with some of the most influential people in the world (no kidding) and asking them questions about their lives and their impact on the planet. It was interesting, to say the least.

Of the twenty-five interviews I did and wrote up, one really stood out. Above all the others, there was one story I got to tell that made me worried and excited and totally honored.

I got to write a bio of Jesus.

The last person in that book full of people who have made a mark on this planet is Jesus Himself. For days I composed sentences and rewrote paragraphs and traded out weak words for stronger synonyms. I've never felt more pressure to write the right thing. This was my chance, the biggest chance I may ever get, to write a bio of the Man who saved my life.

I know that sounds crazy and maybe super Christian-y, but let me tell you this: if you knew all the things that Jesus had rescued me from, all the ways that He is my Savior and my healer, you would understand. He has saved me in every sense of the word. For real. So to write about Him—the Man who is also my hero and my best friend—well, it was indescribable.

I love to talk about Jesus. I haven't always, but I do now. I really love to talk about Him because I know Him. This verse, that I've already shared with you but want you to see again, moves me because I feel the truth deep inside.

1 PETER 1:8-9 (**THE MESSAGE**)

> You never saw him, yet you love him. You still don't see him, yet you trust him—with laughter and singing. Because you kept on believing, you'll get what you're looking forward to: total salvation.

But growing up, the pressure to talk about Jesus to my friends, especially my non-Christian friends, felt heavy. I missed a key factor about sharing the gospel: it's about love. When you love someone, you talk about that person. Two of my favorite humans are Connor and Keenan, two college guys from our church. I could talk about them all day long—how great they are at life and baseball and loving God and telling jokes and eating a lot of food—because I love them. I could talk for hours about my family or about my best friends Haley and Molly. Because I love them.

And that's how it is with Jesus—He's easy to talk about when you love Him.

At the same time, I know sharing the Gospel of Jesus Christ can be hard and intimidating and strange. So here's how this is gonna roll. I sat down with some of my friends recently and we talked about what it is like to share the gospel. We came up with a list of questions that people ask when they want to talk about Jesus but don't know exactly how to go about it.

What if I Don't Know Him?

That's a great starter question. There is a chance you've gotten this far in the book and you actually aren't a Christian yourself. Well done, I say to you, for not quitting this book. I'm glad you kept reading. I hope you can see from what you've read so far that this Jesus guy is the real deal—He has changed me, saved me, and still rescues my heart all the time.

Having a relationship with Jesus isn't always easy. He didn't promise us that the Christian life would be trouble free. In fact, in John 16:33 Jesus said, "In this world you will have trouble. But take heart! I have overcome the world."

John 3:16 says it all. God loves you so much that He gave up His own Son so that your sin would not be able to separate you from Him forever. God is holy and we are sinners. But Jesus bridged that gap; His death and resurrection cleared that path. And all we have to do is believe it. Believe that Jesus died for your sins and was resurrected and wants to be a part of your life.

If you've never done that before, and you feel this thing deep in your knower that is telling you the truth of who He is and that He loves you, pray this prayer.

Dear Jesus,

Thank You for dying for my sins. Forgive me for all the ways that I have messed up in the past, and the ways I will surely mess up in the future. I want You in my life—I want You to take over my life. You are welcome here, Jesus. In my heart. In my life. To cover my past and orchestrate my future. Change me.

That's it.

ROMANS 10:9

If you confess with your mouth, "Jesus is Lord," and believe in your heart that God raised him from the dead, you will be saved.

You will be saved. From hell? Yes. But from so much more. Abundant life isn't just the eternal life—it's here. It's now. Living with Jesus is the greatest adventure. Buckle up, because even on the hard days this is a great life.

Why Should I Share the Gospel?

Well, the main message of Christianity starts here. We are all sinners and we deserve death. The gift of Jesus's death and resurrection rescues us from that death and gives us eternal life. Christians, those who have accepted the free gift from God, will spend eternity with Him. But those who don't will spend eternity separated from God.

Not good.

So you should be willing to tell your friends about Jesus because you want them to experience the beauty that will be eternity with God, where there are streets of gold and no more tears and lots of other incredibly awesome things. Check out Revelation 21 to see what eternity will be like. (Eternity is a hard thing for my brain to understand, but someday it will make tons of sense. I promise.)

But on another level, you should share the gospel—the story of Jesus and what He has done for us all—because of the difference He makes in your life here and now.

Remember John 10:10. While Satan only plans to destroy, Jesus came so that we could have a full life now. I want my friends and family to know the freedom from guilt that comes with forgiveness from God. I want them to know the peace of making a decision knowing that God will take care of them. I want them to feel the love that God has for us, displayed in what Jesus did.

It's about eternal life, yes. But it's about today too.

And the last words recorded from Jesus show how important it was to Him that we tell others.

MATHEW 28:19-20

Go and make disciples of all nations, baptizing them in the name of the Father and of the Son and of the Holy Spirit, and teaching them to obey everything I have commanded you. And surely I am with you always, to the very end of the age.

When you love someone, you can't resist telling others about Him, remember? We get the privilege of sharing the gospel, the story of the One who loves us the most. We are lucky.

Where Do I Start?

You start with your story. No compelling documentary begins with the facts; they always begin with story. Story is powerful. (Read Donald Miller's *A Million Miles in a Thousand Years* and you'll understand why.) Start there. Start with what you know— talk about the day you got saved.

I remember my salvation story clearly. It was a Sunday in May—May 4, 1986 to be exact. I was almost six years old and I was sitting about three-quarters of the way toward the back of the church in a pew on the left side. I don't remember what the preacher was saying, but I remember feeling this thing inside—this thing that made my heart expand. I looked up to my mother, on my right, and I said, "I think I'm supposed to go up there." So we did. My mom and dad and I went to the altar and the pastor walked me through a similar prayer to the one I wrote for you above.

I've had hard seasons and lots of questions since that day, but I knew the decision I made and I meant it.

THAT'S where you start. You start with where He found you.

How Do I Tell Someone About Jesus?

Honest answer? There are lots of ways. For many of us, the majority of people in our lives have at least heard of Jesus, right? There are millions of people on the planet who have never heard the story of Jesus and what He did for humankind, but most of the people in my life? They have heard of Him.

When I lived in Scotland, we would meet students at the local universities and invite them around to our events, whether that was a chili cook-off, evening service, or dinner together followed by watching *Downton Abbey*. After that initial night, if a new gal came to hang with us, I would see if she wanted to get coffee later that week. That was my job: connect with new students and make them feel welcome in our church family. (I loved it. One of the best jobs I've ever had.) The Starbucks in my Edinburgh neighborhood was an easy walk from the bus stop and just across Morningside Road from the Eric Liddell Centre, where our church met.

For most of the girls, when I met them I had no idea where they were in their faith walk. Had they heard of Jesus? Did they know who He was? Had they heard the gospel before and decided not to believe? Or were they sure of their faith?

So we would sit down—me with a soy chai and peach muffin, them usually with some sort of delicious mocha coffee concoction—and the conversation would start casually. Why we were both in Edinburgh, what their family was like, how they were adjusting to college. We would tell stories.

Once the stories quieted, I would just say, "So tell me what you think about God."

It's way easier to know what to say about Jesus if you know what someone already thinks. And listen, don't stress about this. Your friend's salvation is NOT in your hands. It's God's kindness that brings people to repentance (Romans 2:4); it's not based on your ability to say all the exactly right things.

The Bible says to always be ready to share about the hope that we have.

1 PETER 3:15

> In your hearts set apart Christ as Lord. Always be prepared to give an answer to everyone who asks you to give the reason for the hope that you have.

I want to be prepared, don't you? When I'm sitting at Starbucks looking into the eyes of a freshman at the University of Edinburgh, I want to share hope with her when she says, "I don't really think about God. I don't need Him." Because she needs Him, I need Him, we all need Him.

I heard my friend Chris Wheeler (chriswheeler.org) give the gospel presentation every weekend at Girls of Grace in 2012, and I was blown away at how easy and straight-forward and true he made it all sound. With his permission, I want you to see how simply true the gospel is when you put it into ten sentences. (He came up with these ten sentences. Impressivo, huh?)

The Gospel in Ten Sentences

1. God is **HOLY**.
2. God **created** the world. (Genesis 1:1)
3. God **created humankind** for His glory. (Genesis 1:26–27)
4. Humanity **sinned** against God and now all are born sinners. (Romans 3:23)
5. Sin **separates** humanity from God, who is HOLY. (John 3:3)

6. Sin **deserves** death and eternal separation from God. (Romans 6:23)
7. Jesus is both **God & Man** . . . God's Son came to earth as a man & lived a sinless life.
8. Jesus **took our punishment** for our sins by dying on the cross. (Romans 5:8, John 3:16, 1 Peter 3:18)
9. Jesus **came back to life** three days later . . . He beat death!
10. Jesus offers forgiveness for our sin as a **free gift** to all who would repent & believe. (1 John 1:9, John 14:6, John 5:24, John 10:10, Romans 10:9–11)

Incredible, right? In just ten sentences, you can share the total of the gospel: what Jesus did and why He did it.

Because sharing the gospel has always felt stressful to me (What if I forget a major part of the story or mess up the theology???), I loved how simple these ten sentences are. So you know what I did? I just wrote them on note cards and memorized them. Not like memorizing for a science test, but really letting these ten sentences sink into me.

When you cover those ten sentences, you are telling the story. You are sharing the gospel.

What If She Doesn't Believe Me?

That's okay. Really. I promise. Remember, it is not your responsibility to "save" her, just to share with her. Most people need to hear the gospel, or be touched by that story, more than once. So maybe as a kid they heard about Jesus, and their grandma gave them a Bible, and then you tell them about Jesus, and THEN they go to Young Life and eventually get saved. Do you see the progression? You never know where you are in your friend's path to Jesus; just trust that you and your words are on that path.

Don't panic. Don't worry. Just continue to love your friend and pray for her and share your stories of faith with her when the opportunities arise.

What If She DOES Believe Me? What Do I Do Next?

You pray with her. Have her pray that same prayer I wrote up at the start of this chapter. You have her ask Jesus to forgive her of her sins and to come into her life. And then you tell somebody. Well, I mean, let HER tell somebody—it's not really your story to share—but encourage her to tell her parents or your youth pastor or a trusted Christian teacher or mentor.

When I was in the seventh grade at summer camp, my friend Julie asked me to sit outside on the back steps of the cabin during our free time for a chat. So we sat there in the hot July sun while she asked me about Jesus and whether He was the real deal. I told her what I knew—that Jesus had changed my life, that He really was the Son of God, and that He had died and rose again to save us from our sins.

She said she wanted to pray that He would come into her life.

I got so scared. I mean SO scared. I was worried that we would pray the wrong thing and it wouldn't count or something. (Dumb. Not possible. Just ask Jesus to forgive you of your sins

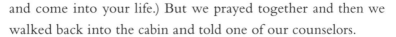

and come into your life.) But we prayed together and then we walked back into the cabin and told one of our counselors.

It was a beautiful day.

What If She Has Questions I Can't Answer?

Guess what? I bet you have questions about faith that I can't answer. And I bet I have questions about faith that you can't answer. And I bet your friend has questions about faith that neither of us can answer.

Here's the ticket—be honest. If she asks you something that stumps you, tell her so. "You know, I'm not totally sure. But I will go ask my youth leader and see what he says."

It's that easy. Don't freak out—your not having all the answers isn't going to ruin anyone's life. If anything, it will remind your friend that you are human and that being a Christian doesn't mean being perfect.

Here's a verse you can share:

PHILIPPIANS 2:12

My dear friends, as you have always obeyed—not only in my presence, but now much more in my absence—continue to work out your salvation with fear and trembling."

All of us, me included, are working out our salvation. Every day we are faced with moments and questions and issues and hurts that don't have easy answers. That's totally fine. Be honest about your struggles, but remember that no matter how bad it gets, YOU HAVE HOPE. Jesus is your hope. And He is what we want to share.

But this is a great reason for you to have a small group leader, youth leader, coach, parent, or teacher in your life you can go to at any point about this stuff. Ask your questions. Her questions. All of it. And listen, why not ask your youth pastor if both you and your friend can meet with him? That way, you can learn the answers to your faith questions together.

What Happens If I Miss a Chance to Share the Gospel?

When I was a sophomore in college, I went to the gym. (I mean, I've been to the gym a few times since then, so I'm not saying that was my LAST time at the gym. Just wanted to make that clear.) Anyway. I was on the stationary bike, reading a Max Lucado book about Jesus. On the cover of the book are nails and a thorn crown. As I read and pedaled and sweated, I noticed the guy next to me kept cutting his eyes toward me. He was checking out the cover of the book, and I felt this thing inside of me. This little push from the Holy Spirit to give him the book. I was so nervous and scared and I was freaking out like, "What if he doesn't want it or what if I flub up the presentation or what if he doesn't like it AT ALL??"

So I pedaled on for another few minutes until the timer on the bike beeped, announcing that I had officially suffered long enough. My feet stopped, but I just sat there. I was too nervous. I practiced in my mind what I wanted to say and finally stood up.

And walked out of the gym.

I passed right by the guy. Carrying my book that I had literally finished reading right there on the bike and knowing that I felt the Holy Spirit pushing me to give it away, I just kept going.

I got in the car with my roommate, who began to play a song by David Crowder. The line that kept repeating? "I will not be silent."

I put my elbows on my knees and dropped my head. I knew I had missed a chance that I was supposed to take. I felt terrible.

I missed the chance to share the gospel.

I'm sure there are other moments I've missed in the last three decades, but that one stands out, and it always will, because I still pray for that man.

You know, in the book of Esther, she is given the opportunity to save the entire Jewish population, her people, but she gets scared and isn't sure she can do it. When she tells her uncle Mordecai that she is scared, his response is interesting.

ESTHER 4:14

If you remain silent at this time, relief and deliverance for the Jews will arise from another place, but you and your father's family will perish. And who knows but that you have come to royal position for such a time as this?

When I miss an open door to share the gospel, God will use someone else. He will make sure that everyone knows about Jesus. When I don't share the gospel, you know who is really missing out? ME. I missed out on being a part of that man's salvation story, the gift of giving, and the blessing of being obedient to God.

If you miss the chance once, don't miss it again. God forgives, God still speaks and directs, but it only takes one experience like mine in the gym to know that I never want to feel that loss again.

Why Do I Feel So Much Pressure?

Maybe you don't feel pressure about sharing the gospel. That's great.

But if you do, and it sometimes makes you feel like you are going to panic because WHAT HAPPENS IF I DON'T TELL HER ABOUT JESUS RIGHT NOW, then you can breathe easy.

I used to feel this too. I know. It can feel like such a heavy burden to think, "My friends need to hear about Jesus and they need to hear about Him from ME." As a high school sophomore, I was a manager for my school's football team. I loved those guys a lot and wanted them to know Jesus soooooo bad. And the pressure of what to say and how to live and what to pray sometimes felt like a massive weight sitting directly on my chest.

That is not from God.

I think you feel pressure for a lot of reasons.

1. You really care about your friend.
2. You don't want her to go to hell.
3. You don't know what to say.

But here is the truth: God is in control. Just like Esther, you GET to be a part of His story; you don't HAVE to be. And remember that it is the Holy Spirit who draws people to Himself (see Romans 2:4)—it is not our job to "make" someone into a Christian.

But certainly, and hear me here, we do have a responsibility to obey God when we feel the push to share. Pressure isn't always bad, because sometimes you need a little nudge to remember why it is important for you to say the brave thing or the hard thing. It's when the pressure starts to cause panic or fear that you need to slow down, pray for God's wisdom and for open doors, and continue to live your life, sharing when you can.

(By the way, if you weren't sure before, now you know what to share. Your story. Ten sentences. Amen. You're good to go, sister.)

My friend Connor made a great point when we were talking about this question. He said, "I think I feel pressure when I focus on sharing what I know in my head instead of what I know in my heart."

Amen to that too. Share what you know in your heart and let the Holy Spirit do the rest.

What Difference Does It Make?

More than you can ever know. God intentionally makes us unaware, I think, of all the ways that our lives affect other people—probably to protect us from the pride of thinking we are the most über-important humans who have ever existed on this planet.

Whether you start one conversation at the lunch table or stand in front of hundreds of teens night after night giving a gospel presentation, you are making a difference.

We assume that the loudest people are the most influential and make the most difference. I disagree.

Last weekend at Girls of Grace, a student asked, "What if I want my words to make an impact but no one is listening?"

Trust me, sister. Someone is listening.

There is a story I heard a few summers ago, a totally true story that has deeply influenced my life. It's the story of the Welsh Revival of 1904. The entire country of Wales was changed—thousands of people accepted Christ as their personal Lord and Savior, entire soccer teams didn't show up to play because they were at church, and jails emptied as criminals stopped committing crimes. (Check the appendix for more resources you can check out about this revival.)

How did the revival start? Check out these details from a first-hand account:

In February 1904, the Spirit of God bade [Pastor Jenkins] introduce some new feature into the young people's meeting held after the morning service, and it dawned on him to ask for testimony, definite testimony, as to what the Lord had done for their own souls.

One or two rose to speak, but it was not testimony. It was just then that the same young girl [named Florrie Evans, who had been afraid to give her life to Christ the night before]—shy, nervous, intelligent—stood up in tears and with clasped hands simply said with a deep pathos, "Oh I love Jesus Christ with all my heart." Instantly, the Spirit of God appears to have fallen upon the gathering . . . It was the beginning of the visible manifestation of the Spirit breaking out in life.

Another report says of the young people who heard her, "their hearts were melted."

Can you dig that? One teen girl. *One* sentence about Jesus. And it sparked a revival in the WHOLE COUNTRY.

Those are some powerful words.

The idea that a teenage girl could utter that one sentence—"I love Jesus Christ with all my heart"—and change an entire country has me absolutely fired up.

That could be you.

It could be me.

We can make a difference with our words about Jesus.

Don't be afraid. Don't be stressed. Don't be worried.

Just be honest, and loving, and open to sharing about the hope that you have. Talk about God, using your words to tell others who He is and what He has done for you.

It only takes a sentence:

I love Jesus Christ with all my heart.

Your Words Matter

Memorize the Word

> In your hearts set apart Christ as Lord. Always be prepared to give an answer to everyone who asks you to give the reason for the hope that you have. But do this with gentleness and respect.
>
> **—1 PETER 3:15**

Read the Word

- 1 Peter 1:8–9
- John 3:16
- Romans 10:9
- John 10:10
- Matthew 28:19–20
- Philippians 2:12
- Esther 4:14
- Revelation 21
- Romans 2:4
- Use your concordance or BibleGateway.com to search this term:
  - salvation

- Have you ever read the story of Jesus? The story of His life can be found in the Bible in Matthew, Mark, Luke, and John. Those stories would be good to read during your times with God. Check online or use the YouVersion app to find a reading plan to read through the Gospels (the first four books of the New Testament).

Journal Your Words

- Write the memory verse in your journal.
- If you can, list a few people in your life who you know need to hear about Jesus.
- Write out the ten sentences from Chris Wheeler that will help you explain the gospel to your friends.
- Do you find it easy or hard to talk about Jesus to your friends? Write out why or why not.
- Journal about what role you think prayer plays in sharing the gospel.

Use Your Words

- Be brave. Ask God to open doors for you to share your faith with someone in your life who needs to hear about Jesus.
- Practice! Call some of your small group girls and y'all get together and practice sharing the gospel with each other. No pressure and tons of practice will make it easier when the opportunity really happens!
- Write out your testimony. When and why did you become a Christian? Tell the whole story with as many details as you can recall.

PART 3

Last but Not Least? You.

Before I release you into a word-filled world, to go and conquer and speak and love and change the atmosphere of every place you step, there's one more girl we need to talk about.

You.

In the last ten years, my capacity to love others has grown exponentially. My ability to appreciate other people and speak life and love into their hearts is greater than ever. I have more friends who love me and more opportunities to talk about Jesus and His love than ever before.

You want to know why?

Because I love me.

Stick with me, I'm not being a nutso. (Though, if you don't think I'm a little loony after reading all this, then I am great at tricking you.)

My first book, *Perfectly Unique*, spends a lot of pages telling you this story. The story of how I used to hate me, and I said so—to myself and to others from time to time—and how God saved me from that mindset and those words. He has changed my mind and heart.

I'm not saying I'm the president of my own fan club or that I am perfect and without flaws. But I am saying that God didn't make a mistake when He made me. I have learned to appreciate all that He has made, and that includes little ol' Annie. And the more I grew to love and appreciate how God made me, I began to see unique opportunities (*perfectly* unique opportunities?) and one-of-a-kind ways that God wanted me to move and act in the world. As I grew to love and know myself better, I better saw my place on this planet. I plugged into those things that make me feel alive. And, as I told you before, I'm having a great time.

I never knew it mattered how I talked to myself. But sister, it does. Oh man, it does.

This section deserves to be read differently. Take your Bible, your journal, and this book and go sit in a comfy place in your house. Maybe put on your slippers and sit under the warmth of your favorite blanket. Set aside some time, maybe on a Saturday, to really dig into this.

It will change everything.

CHAPTER 11

Believe Truth

Your word is a lamp to my feet and a light for my path.

—PSALM 119:105

Iremember when my mom quit doing my laundry. I was in the eighth grade. She quit because I wouldn't put my clothes in the dirty clothes hamper and then take the basket down the stairs to the laundry room.

I often wonder: How long would she have washed and dried my clothes had I just followed that one simple instruction? Would my mother STILL be doing my laundry? Maybe. (But probably not, since, you know, I live in a different city than she does now.)

Once I was in charge of my own clean clothes situation, I decided to label my closet. Sure, I was the only one using said closet, but I found it important to add labels. I sat at my little white desk and cut printer paper into strips, and using markers, I wrote "dresses," "skirts," "khakis," etc. There were about eight different categories, and I taped the labels in my closet. Believe me when I say I was militant about putting things under the exact right label.

I'm a fan of labels.

When I taught elementary school, every drawer and cubby and shared space had a label. Paper clips here, books there, tissues here, homework over there.

Labels are all around us. In restaurants, in stores, in schools. And even on people.

When I think about myself, a few labels come to mind.

Daughter.

Sister.

Girl.

Small Group Leader.

Author.

Mentor.

Friend.

But those aren't the only labels we believe. As if you haven't figured this out yet, I am a big believer in the power of words— the words that other people say about you, the words that you think about yourself, and the words that God says about you— and the power they carry.

If we want to use our words well to speak love to other people, we have to choose to believe true labels about ourselves first.

And I haven't always done that. When I was in high school, I used other labels too.

Ugly.

Fat.

Unloved.

Annoying.

Too much.

Less than.

And when I believed those labels, I acted them out. A favorite pastor of mine, Mark Fritchman, taught us this saying when I was in college:

Watch your thoughts; they become words.

Watch your words; they become actions.

Watch your actions; they become habits.

Watch your habits; they become your character.

Watch your character; it becomes your destiny.

You see, what enters your mind—the labels you believe— becomes who you are, and the labels affect the words you use.

So whether it is labels that the outside world puts on you or labels that are whispered into your head, learn to identify which ones are lies and meant to hurt you and which ones are truth.

Here's a beautiful thing: Jesus changes our labels. Jesus used His words throughout the Bible to counter the lies people believed, to look at the old labels and change them.

In Luke 19, we meet a guy called Zacchaeus. (I know, you gals who grew up in children's church are already singing the song: "Zacchaeus was a wee little man . . .") He's a tax collector, a short little guy who is not too well liked by his neighbors. In fact, in Luke 19:7, all the people start whispering about Zacchaeus and calling him a sinner.

He's labeled. Sinner. Bad guy. Less than.

But Jesus? Jesus sees Zacchaeus, perched up in a tree, and invites Himself over to Zac's house. The amazing thing is what happens next.

LUKE 19:7–10

All the people saw this and began to mutter, "He has gone to be the guest of a 'sinner.'"

But Zacchaeus stood up and said to the Lord, "Look, Lord! Here and now I give half of my possessions to the poor, and if I have cheated anybody out of anything, I will pay back four times the amount."

Jesus said to him, "Today salvation has come to this house, because this man, too, is a son of Abraham. For the Son of Man came to seek and to save what was lost."

Do you see it? Jesus changed Zacchaeus's label, and it changed the words Zacchaeus said. No longer was he the bad guy or the crook, because Jesus called him something new. And something true.

Remember our boy Peter from the beginning of the book? Well, in Matthew 16, his name is Simon.

MATTHEW 16:13–18 (**THE MESSAGE**)

When Jesus arrived in the villages of Caesarea Philippi, he asked his disciples, "What are people saying about who the Son of Man is?"

They replied, "Some think he is John the Baptizer, some say

Elijah, some Jeremiah or one of the other prophets."

He pressed them, "And how about you? Who do you say I am?"

Simon Peter said, "You're the Christ, the Messiah, the Son of the living God."

Jesus came back, "God bless you, Simon, son of Jonah! You didn't get that answer out of books or from teachers. My Father in heaven, God himself, let you in on this secret of who I really am. And now I'm going to tell you who you are, *really* are. You are Peter, a rock. This is the rock on which I will put together my church, a church so expansive with energy that not even the gates of hell will be able to keep it out.

His name is Simon, but Jesus calls him Peter and says he is a "rock." And although Peter messed up with his words (haven't we all?), you can follow him through the New Testament and see how God used him to build the church—that same church you are a part of now.

Jesus changed Peter's name, his label. And Peter used his words to change the world.

So you see, even people in the Bible had labels that were wrong until Jesus spoke and changed their identities to something true. There are many more examples, like in John 8 when a woman was caught in adultery and Jesus set her free and told her to sin no more. She was caught, but He let her go. That's a new label. A new word.

To believe Truth, to speak in love and truth, we have to recognize that every label we believe about ourselves isn't necessarily true. And we have to listen to Jesus, to His words, and let HIM define us.

Breaking the Cycle

Satan is a liar. I know you know that, but I want to say it again. He is a liar. He wants to define you, label you, and stop you from using your words to change the world.

When he lies to you (for instance, "You are ugly"), you begin to swirl that thought around in your head: "I guess I am ugly, she is prettier than me, I'm definitely the ugliest girl in our class." Soon ugly words to yourself lead to ugly words about others ("Did you see her outfit today? Woof.") only because you are hurting and insecure.

You hear a lie, you treat it like truth, it becomes a label, and then you act out of that label.

It's a vicious cycle that can only be treated by a heaping dose of Truth—the real stuff. That's why I love the Bible. In the Bible, God has already given you all the labels you need, and that's how we learn how to treat ourselves and each other.

When I was in high school, one of the older women in our church came to our small group one night to teach on "standards." I know, I know. Roll your eyes like I did, because I was so tired of hearing how I was supposed to dress and what I was supposed to look like as a Christian. But she did a very interesting thing—she took us to twelve verses in the Bible and said, "Look, here is what God says is your standard for how you are to live."

It was like it was all laid out right there for me. How were we supposed to dress? 1 Peter 3 says that our beauty shouldn't come from what is on the outside, but what is on the inside. At each verse, she'd say, "Write here, beside the verse, that this is your standard for clothing." And I did. That same Bible goes with me everywhere, fifteen years later, so I can still see the words "standard of clothing" written in blue pen beside those underlined verses.

I was glad that she came to our group that night. I learned that I didn't have to decide for myself how I was supposed to live and I also didn't necessarily have to listen to the people who I felt were being bossy about my life. I just had to look to the Bible to decide how to be.

And that is still true.

When I struggle with labels—and listen, I still STRUGGLE with labels and choosing to believe what the Bible says about me instead of what I hear in my head—I turn to the Bible.

Sounds like the cheesy Christian answer, right? Well, let me prove that while you may think it's cheesy, it is also totally true and awesome. Listen, the Bible is THE authority on who we are and how we are to live. It is our guide.

PSALM 119:105

Your word is a lamp to my feet and a light for my path.

God's Word is meant to light up the dark places, to invade those corners full of lies and shine beams of truth. When light enters, darkness flees. And the only way we can shine light into the world is if the light lives in us.

This is the same reason that I've encouraged you to memorize a verse every single chapter. Because we should have God's Word stored up deep in our hearts, so that when we hear the lies and they try to suck us back into the darkness, we can combat them. Immediately.

Sister, you *have* to fight the lies. I know it is hard. I know. I KNOW.

If you only knew how many times I said ugly things to myself on a daily basis and then had to take them back and say, "No, Annie. That is not true. You are loved and cared for, and God is on your side and He made you on purpose."

Sometimes, even if you are being tortured, it is easier to relax into the pain than to fight it. But you have to fight it. You were meant to change the world with your words, and the enemy wants to do all he can to steal, kill, and destroy you into silence.

Don't. Be. Silent.

A girl believing lies but trying to share the truth is like a flashlight in need of batteries.

Let's get some batteries.

The Labels that Matter

This is the process that I've found to believing Truth. (In *Perfectly Unique*, I talk about Lie/Truth cards, and this is that same idea, only with the added step of thinking through how believing the truth can affect the words you say. So check out the Mind chapter of *Perfectly Unique* if you want to dig deeper into this.) And you'll see, in the examples below, why it is important to know Scripture to get to be the kind of woman you want to be.

LIE: You hear that you are ugly.
TRUTH: God says you are beautiful. (Song of Songs 4:7)
RESULT: If you choose to believe Him, you grow to love yourself and the way that God made you, and then you are able to love other people with more of your heart.

LIE: You see someone being bullied and you think, "I

can't do anything because I don't want to fight this battle by myself." You hear that you are alone.

TRUTH: God says He fights for us. (Exodus 14:14)

RESULT: If you choose to believe Him, you stand up for your friend, knowing that God fights on your side and that you are not alone.

LIE: You hear that you have no future. That because of your upbringing or your neighborhood or your family situation or your lot in life, God doesn't have good plans for you.

TRUTH: God says He does. God says that He has great plans for you. (Jeremiah 29:11)

RESULT: If you choose to believe Him, you live with hope and look to the future with excitement and can encourage others to do the same, no matter what has happened in their history.

LIE: You hear that no one loves you.

TRUTH: God says He does. (Jeremiah 31:3)

RESULT: If you choose to believe Him, you live like someone who is loved. You speak with kindness and a lightness because you know that no matter what, you are deeply loved.

LIE: You hear that you are a sinner, you have screwed up too much.

TRUTH: God says He knew that you would screw up, and He loved you anyway. (Romans 5:8)

RESULT: If you choose to believe Him, you can live

openly and honestly, without guilt or shame, and use your words to show others about God's forgiveness.

LIE: You hear that you don't matter to anyone.
TRUTH: God says He bought you. You cost Him something of great worth—His Son. He thinks you have great value. (1 Corinthians 6:20)
RESULT: If you choose to believe Him, when your friend says she wants to commit suicide because she doesn't matter to anyone, you can tell her with assurance that she matters a great deal to you and to God.

We could keep going and going. The Bible is full of the amazing things God says about you.

The challenge isn't finding the verses—thanks to the Internet and websites like BibleGateway.com, all you have to do is search "verses about how God feels about me" and for the next thirty minutes you can be reading them.

The challenge? The challenge is believing them.

It's way easier to believe you are ugly when you see what "beauty" is according to our culture or when you don't love the way your clothes fit. The old labels are tough to lose, I know. The battle to believe truth is a daily one in which some days will feel simple and others will be heartbreakingly hard.

Listen, you think I don't feel alone in this battle to speak love to you so that you will speak it to others? The lies I hear EVERY DAY tell me that I am alone in this, the only soldier in an army fighting to free you from lies and set you free to speak truth to the people in your world. Sometimes I feel like all I want to do is throw my computer into the street and crawl into bed.

But God reminds me. He fights for me. He is with me. I am not alone.

I choose to believe Him because I know He is right. So I keep fighting, even when the battle is just words on a page. And when I believe Him, I use my words to say so. See how that works?

Four Ways to Defeat the Lies

So how do you beat the lies?

1. Get some people on your team.

Whether it is your small group friends, your parents or another adult, your leaders at church, or an older girl in your life, you've got to have some other people helping you identify lies.

Anytime I say something negative about myself out loud, one of my best friends, Nichole, will say, "Um, please don't talk about my friend that way." The first few times, it confused me. And then I realized—Nichole wouldn't let me talk about any of our *other* friends that way, so she wasn't going to let me talk about myself that way either.

Your people can help you identify the lies and replace them with the truth.

2. Get to know the Truth.

The Bible, sister. You need to know it. You need to know the truth so that you can identify it up against a lie. If you hear anything in your head that doesn't agree with the Word of God, it is a lie. Plain and simple.

A lie I used to struggle with was that God loved other people more than He loved me. When I shared this with a friend in college, she showed me these verses.

ACTS 10:34–35

Then Peter began to speak: "I now realize how true it is that God does not show favoritism but accepts men from every nation who fear him and do what is right."

So I called on my team to help me know the Truth so that I didn't live under that lie of a label.

The Bible is full of words that speak straight to our hearts like this, and stories that show us examples of other humans who have dealt with some of the same stuff we are facing.

(Sometimes it is hard to know where to start. Check the appendix for a few other resources that I've found helpful when trying to live in Truth.)

3. And repeat.

The Bible says that when you know the Truth, it will set you free (see John 8:32). The better you know the Truth, the freer you are. Yes and amen. So read it, memorize it, go over it and over it again. Write important verses on note cards and hang them on your bathroom mirror. The verse I'm working on memorizing right now? (I'm gonna try to do it without looking. I'll let you know how it goes . . .)

HOSEA 10:12

Sow for yourselves righteousness, reap the fruit of unfailing love, and break up your unplowed ground; for it is time to seek the Lord, until he comes and showers righteousness on you.

(I did it, by the way, except I missed some punctuation. So I'd say 97 percent correct.)

Especially as you identify labels that you have lived under, you need to find and memorize and repeat those verses that remind you what is true.

For example, when I hear in my head that I am too much or not enough (both tend to come into my brain on a fairly regular basis), I've learned enough of Psalm 139 that I can say it to myself. I am fearfully and wonderfully made. And that's the truth.

4. Teach It and Tell It.

The best way to understand anything is to get involved! As a college student, I taught my church's high school Sunday school class with my friend Kevin. While it was a real season of growth for me spiritually, I would say that the lessons that are still with me today are the ones that I taught to those students every other week (assuming I didn't accidentally oversleep. It happened).

So how do you do that? Well, it could be as simple as sharing what you are learning with your siblings or your friends at lunch. A few weeks ago, Sonnie and Betsy and I got coffee on a Sunday afternoon. We weren't planning on talking about anything serious, we just wanted to catch up. As the afternoon wore on, we went from telling simple funny stories to discussing profound things that we were learning from God and other people. We didn't set out to "teach" each other per se, but that just happens sometimes. When you talk about what God is doing for you, other people learn from it. (Remember—that's why we share our stories first.)

But there are also real opportunities to teach that you

should look into. Does your school have an FCA (Fellowship of Christian Athletes) group? Maybe you could teach that one week. Or Young Life or youth group or your small group. It'll take you having a little courage and a little umph to get a chance to teach what you are learning, but go for it!

Another option? ONLINE, SISTER! Blog what you are learning, tweet the verses you are memorizing, or write a Facebook post about new truths in your heart. Remember, you never know how many people are going to be impacted by what you share online. (It's beautiful and a bit terrifying, yes?)

Share the truth as it hides in your heart. Never be ashamed of what you are learning, even if you are in process. It's a beautiful thing to share in the middle of the lesson—you don't have to wait until the end!

Christ Has Set You Free

It's a choice. Believing truth is always a choice. In every situation, in every conversation, and in every moment you stand in front of a mirror and begin to criticize yourself, you have the choice to fight for truth or give into the lies.

There is so much power when you begin to understand that you are who GOD says you are, not who other people say you are or who your mind believes you are.

You're free from those labels, my friend. The only labels you have to hold on to are the ones that remind you that you are loved and cherished and beautiful.

Let me tell you about believing in Truth and how it changed my life.

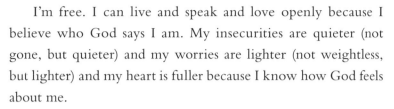

I'm free. I can live and speak and love openly because I believe who God says I am. My insecurities are quieter (not gone, but quieter) and my worries are lighter (not weightless, but lighter) and my heart is fuller because I know how God feels about me.

I am released to believe that I am who He says I am. That the Bible is true. That I am deeply loved no matter what.

I'm not perfect, but I have the freedom to be right or wrong or successful or not.

You can too, friend. Really. You can. This isn't something special for me and me alone because I'm an author or an adult or a Nashville resident. This is for you too.

Freedom from lies is for all of us.

GALATIANS 5:1 (THE MESSAGE)

Christ has set us free to live a free life. So take your stand! Never again let anyone put a harness of slavery on you.

Start today. Don't wait. I wonder if your heart has been just waiting for permission to fight, to stand up and refute the lies that try to take over your mind. In your comfy place, wherever that is, take some time and think about the labels that try to define you, think about the lies that try to divert you from the course God has planned, and look for the truth that should be your identification.

Read this chapter again if you need to, really. Digest it. Feel it. Ask God to change you through it. This can change the whole course of your life and the direction of your words.

Believe the truth. Fight the lies. Everything will change.

Your Words Matter

Memorize the Word

> Your word is a lamp to my feet and a light for my path.
>
> —PSALM 119:105

Read the Word

- Luke 19
- Matthew 16
- 1 Peter 3
- Song of Songs 4:7
- Exodus 14:14
- Jeremiah 29:11
- Jeremiah 31:3
- Romans 5:8
- 1 Corinthians 6:20
- Acts 10:34–35
- Hosea 10:12
- Galatians 5:1

Journal Your Words

- Make a list of the labels that you feel like have been placed on you. Circle the ones that you think may be lies.
- What lies do you know you currently believe?
- Write out a prayer to God asking Him to reveal to you anything you believe that isn't true.
- Find some Scriptures that will help combat the lies and help you embrace the truth.

Use Your Words

- Talk to someone else in your life—a friend or mentor—about the lies you are believing. Let him or her help you identify truths to fight against those lies.
- Write out some Scriptures that are truths you need in your heart, and hang the verses in your room or bathroom or on your car's dashboard or in your locker.
- Post your favorite new verse on social media and hashtag #SpeakLove.
- Settle into this chapter, don't rush it. There's a lot to be learned here and digested, so take your time and really work through what you believe about yourself and what labels need to go.

CHAPTER 12

Love You

For out of the overflow of the heart the mouth speaks.

—MATTHEW 12:34

When people and preachers are trying to teach us how to treat other people, whether in word or action, there are some verses that always get tossed into the mix. And they are verses I like. Seriously. But I wonder how well we really know them. They have stung me a time or two, when I realized what they were really asking of me. It's not just about other people. It's about me too.

MATTHEW 22:34-40

Hearing that Jesus had silenced the Sadducees, the Pharisees got together. One of them, an expert in the law, tested him with

> this question: "Teacher, which is the greatest commandment in the Law?"
>
> Jesus replied: "'Love the Lord your God with all your heart and with all your soul and with all your mind.' This is the first and greatest commandment. And the second is like it: 'Love your neighbor as yourself.' All the Law and the Prophets hang on these two commandments."

In high school, my mind was full of evil whispers of how unlovely I was, how much I needed to change, and how God had messed up when He made me. I didn't know then that I could call those whispers "lies," so I let them fester and grow until they were kudzu covering my soul. And I lived like that, in self-hatred, for years.

Why didn't I just talk about it? It's a question I've rolled around in my mind for years. In the end, I think the truth is that I didn't reveal the things in my head because I didn't know that I had a choice to think of them as anything but truth. It wasn't until later that I learned to distinguish lies from truth and believe the labels God puts on me. My teen years were the classic story of someone eating a mud pie because they didn't realize they were sitting in the yard of a bakery.

(Dessert talk is so distracting. Back to high school stories.)

Once during my sophomore year, my mom was taking me home from soccer practice and asked me a pointed question: "How do you think you can love your friends if you don't love yourself?"

I was puzzled. "Who cares if I love me?" I thought. I

remember genuinely considering that my mother did not know what she was talking about.[1]

(Shocking no mom ever, a teenager thought she knew best.)

She didn't push me, she just let me mull her question over in my mind. I don't know that I even answered her; if I did, it was something teen-angsty, like, "Uh, Mom, you don't even understand how much I love my friends and I love God, and that's all that matters." And then I probably got out of the minivan and took my sweaty soccer self and sat on her beautiful couch, waiting for her to cook dinner for our family. (So what I'm saying is, I was a real pleasure as a teen.)

That conversation has stuck with me for all these years. And as I grew up, and God rescued me from many of those lies and taught me how to fight for truth, I realized (gasp) that my mother was right.

While we are capable of loving others to some degree even when we are drowning in self-hate, there is a freedom in love that comes with following the second-greatest commandment.

Do you love yourself? Do you see yourself the way God sees you? Do you recognize how absolutely loveable you are? Because when you do, when you see all that truth, you can't help loving your neighbor.

To love someone is to believe in them. When someone believes in you, it changes everything—how you carry yourself, how you treat others, how you live day after day. You can give that same gift to those around you.

---

1   Bizarrely, this is also the same curve in the road where my mom told me to start waxing my eyebrows. Apparently, she got very inspired to improve her children while on this stretch of the street.

Feel the Love

This section gets real personal and all up in my business. I bet it feels the same for you. Sure, it's hard to talk about the mean girl and how to spend time listening to God, but things seem to get more raw and intense when we are talking about those quiet moments of self-dislike.

But here's the thing. Those verses at the beginning of the chapter? THAT. IS. TRUE. My mom was right: you have to love yourself to love others well. Jesus said it Himself—love others AS you love yourself. That's something worth thinking through.

I would never claim to have every answer to every question, but when it comes to moving from self-hatred to a true appreciation of how God has made me, I'm a bit of a seasoned expert. Trust me, I've looped through that cycle more times than I can count, including this morning when I did not like the look of the jeans I put on and told myself so. Old Annie would have continued a barrage of ugly remarks about my looks, but instead I looked in the mirror and said, "Hey, put on a different pair. No biggie." And I shook it off and moved on.

(Listen, I know I talk out loud to myself a lot. But you know what? When it is the difference between living under the weight of those slimy lies or living in the light freedom of truth, I'll talk to myself for that. You would too.)

I'd like to insert a caveat here: you can only love because Christ loved you first.

1 JOHN 4:19

We love because he first loved us.

See, it's not that you are intrinsically good and deserve to be loved—remember that at our core, we are all sinners in need of a Savior. It's not that you have earned the love of God or that you deserve to love yourself because you are so perfect at being a person.

Quite the opposite.

God loves us, even when we don't deserve it.

1 JOHN 4:10

This is love: not that we loved God, but that he loved us and sent his Son as an atoning sacrifice for our sins.

So the caveat is this—you haven't earned this love, it's a gift. We don't attempt to beat the lies and believe the truth and love ourselves because we are perfect. We do it because in our imperfections, God loves us deeply and has made us just the way He wanted.

One of my favorite vloggers (yes, I have favorite vloggers—don't you?) is Hank Green. One time, Hank said, "We are all differently broken, semi-functional, rusted-out love machines." And I think that's right.

Speaking love is about you too. It's not just outward; it's inward. It's realizing that we are broken and rusted out and yet still loved and able to love.

So I humbly present these thoughts on loving yourself, knowing that this topic is sensitive and slow and broad and possibly painful. You may have a billion other ideas on what it looks like to really love you. That's great—go for it. I'm just sharing the ones I know have worked for me.

1. Speak kindly to yourself.

Even on the hard days, that's the first step. Use your words to speak life. Remember how Proverbs 18:21 says everything you say is either producing life or death? It's just as true when you talk to yourself. Just like with my jeans this morning, I have to choose words of life over words of death.

Quit being a mean girl to yourself. Seriously. If we are out to end that pandemic, it has to start here. Inside. At the core of you. If you are going to be the girl who speaks life and develops beautiful things in others with her words, it begins with doing that for yourself to yourself.

Simply said, if we aren't going to stand any longer for the mean girl to exist in our schools and churches and teams and neighborhoods, we can't let her exist in our heads either.

Self-talk is a big part of everyone's life. We constantly, and subconsciously, have thoughts running through our minds that direct our days. You need to listen to those. The negative ones? The ones that cut you down and make you feel unloved? Time to chuck them. Stop yourself, identify the lie, and say the truth in its place.

2. Speak kindly about yourself to others.

While you shouldn't be that girl who talks about herself all the time, you also don't want to be that girl who says, "Uh, well, that dress looks amazing on you but would look disgusting on me." There's no need to tear yourself down. You would never say (I hope), "Uh, that dress looks AMAZING on ME but would look DISGUSTING on YOU." You wouldn't say anything like that to someone else. So why would you say that to yourself?

And this is a great thing to hold your friends accountable to as well—just like my friend Nichole does to me when she tells me, "Don't talk about my friend that way." Accountability doesn't always feel good, but when done in love, calling your friends out of lies and into Truth is the kindest thing you can do.

I think this also should affect the lyrics we sing. When you sing, you are proclaiming things about yourself or someone else. That's why worship music is so powerful—you are focusing on truths about God, words set to music, out loud. For example, I like to listen to Meredith Andrews's album *Worth It All*. Every song on there will challenge how you live. "Start With Me" says:

> You're still the God of the empty tomb
> The One who came to life again
> So come alive in me.

Those are some serious words. Then she sings,

> My life is an empty cup, fill it up.
> I wanna hear every rescued heart cry,
> "You're enough, You're enough"
> Break what needs breaking
> 'til You're all we see
> Start with me. Start with me.

I mean, y'all. If we sing those words out loud about ourselves, God will change our lives.

On the other hand, so many songs we sing have deadly lyrics. I think of one pop song that says, "I'm a hazard to myself, don't let me get me . . ." And so on. Why are you singing THAT stuff over your life? No good, amiga.

I'm not going to sit here and tell you to delete all the music you listen to that isn't worship music. I'm not that girl. But I will tell you that if you are trying to love yourself well and stand guard over the words you say, the songs you sing are a part of that too.

3. Believe the Truth.

Do I need to go there again? Read the last chapter. Again. Until something sinks past the insecurities and lies and settles into the bottom of your knower and plants itself there.

EVERYTHING changes when you believe truth. Everything.

4. Walk with confidence.

Strut, sister. Really. You are so loved. You are God's priority. You have nothing to fear or feel insecure about.

I know, I know. Easy to say, harder to do when you are being picked on or not picked at all. But that's the truth you have to let seep into every area of you. Trust me, I still feel left out and overlooked and unloved some days. We all do. But deep in me, the truth lives and breathes and speaks louder.

So I stand tall. I mean, as tall as a 5'6" girl can stand. But I do. Whether I'm married or single or size 0 or size 22 or have too much hair or cut my bangs too short, I am loved. I am treasured. I am confident.

PSALM 27:1–3

The Lord is my light and my salvation—whom shall I fear? The Lord is the stronghold of my life—of whom shall I be afraid?

When evil men advance against me to devour my flesh, when my enemies and my foes attack me, they will stumble and fall.

Though an army besiege me, my heart will not fear; though war break out against me, even then will I be confident.

Even then. Be confident.

5. Take care of yourself.

This looks different for everyone. And I am certainly *not* telling you to eat a certain way or be a certain size or wear a certain brand or go to a certain college (though I am deeply partial to the SEC, particularly my alma mater the University of Georgia). You know your body and what your body needs, and you need to take care of it. If you love you, then you should love this shell that God has made to house your beautiful soul.

I love getting my eyebrows waxed. I haven't always. In fact, it wasn't until college that I realized I didn't want to have bushy eyebrows or, ahem, a mustache. (Don't judge me—I'm just being honest with you.) So as I grew to love me, I began to take better care of myself, which for me involves waxing areas that I don't want to be hairy. (I never thought writing the word *hairy* in my book would make me feel squeamish, but it does. Sorry if it makes you feel the same.)

On the other hand? The more I grew to love me the less I dyed my hair. For most of high school, all of college, and a few years after, I colored my hair every shade under the sun and some

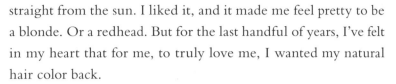

straight from the sun. I liked it, and it made me feel pretty to be a blonde. Or a redhead. But for the last handful of years, I've felt in my heart that for me, to truly love me, I wanted my natural hair color back.

Does that mean you have to wax your eyebrows and stop dying your hair? Absolutely not. You can dye your hair like a rainbow and have the most beautiful unibrow in the world. I totally don't care. But YOU need to decide what things make you feel pretty and loved.

There's a saying that my stylist friend Amber reminds me of often—"Look good, feel good." I don't want it to be true; I wait around a lot trying to *feel* good about me and then hope that translates into *looking* good. But many professionals say it is the other way around.

Within the last year, loving myself the way God loves me has taken an entirely new turn. I have a disease (Polycystic Ovarian Syndrome) that can be controlled and helped greatly by eating a healthy diet. I've known for years—I mean, like EIGHT years—that I had this disease, but I hate dieting so much that I have always ignored it, even though this disease is pretty serious and can lead to *really* serious issues in the future.

(By the way, you should hate dieting too. The diet industry is the worst. Check the appendix for some resources if you want to read more about the freedom to eat healthy without being in bondage to dieting.)

And then, one Saturday in January, I sat at brunch in front of a pile of bananas foster pancakes with some of my best gals. Kelley began to talk about her chronic illness and the way that eating healthily had healed her body.

It was like my eyes were opened for the first time.

I have a disease. I can control that disease. And yet I choose not to because . . . what? Because I'm lazy and don't want to miss out on pancakes?

But God spoke loudly to my heart that day through Kelley. I realized that loving me required treating my body the way it needs to be treated, even if that means missing out on some things. Like pancakes. Sigh.

At the suggestion of my doctor, I am now dairy free. Yes, I miss cheese like I would miss Twitter if it went away (meaning A LOT), but I know what love looks like here. And this is the right thing to do.

And you know what? I feel better than I've felt in years. My outsides and my insides continue to heal and I know that the next step of loving me was treating my body well.

It's not about following rules—you don't have to be like me. It's about hearing God on what loving you looks like. Whether it is saving your babysitting money to buy a nice pair of boots or going to a Zumba class or having a friend teach you how to curl your hair, there are things you can do to show love to yourself.

You only get one body, friend. Love it. Treat it well. Don't harm it with cuts or bruises, don't destroy it with drugs and alcohol, don't give it away to get love, don't abuse it with gluttonous eating. Instead, embrace it, find what makes you feel good about you, and go for it! (Remember: Confidence. Look good, feel good.)

6. Do the things you like.

At a retreat a few weeks ago, I did a Q&A that ended with a student asking me what is the one thing I wish I would have known as a ninth grader. That's one of the easiest questions I've ever answered.

I wish I would have known that I could like anything I wanted to like.

I loved playing in the middle school band. I've always been a huge music fan. In fact, I taught myself to play the piano by using a tiny three-octave electric keyboard and a hymnal that my choir director gave us at the end of the school year in third grade. So when I entered middle school, I immediately joined the band. It was a tough choice between band and orchestra, because I couldn't decide between the French horn and the cello. While my friend and neighbor Grace joined the orchestra, I felt the pull to the French horn. And boy, did I love that thing.

When it was time to go to high school, though, I quit because I thought it was uncool to be in the band. My self-esteem was so low that I gave up something I really enjoyed because I was working so hard to be perceived as cool.

If I had really loved me then, I would have kept playing the French horn and probably would have really enjoyed it. Maybe I'd be performing in the Nashville Symphony now instead of just wondering if I even remember how to play the instrument. But I thought it was more important to do the "cool thing" than to do the thing I loved—I needed everyone else's approval since I didn't have my own.

But listen. To truly love yourself gives you permission to do the thing you want to do, to like whatever *you* want to like.

Remember my friend Anne from the chapter about our online life? The one who made friends through Tumblr? Anne gets this. She is into the stuff she is into because she genuinely likes it, not because someone else decided it was cool. And I think that's awesome.

That's my hope for you. That as you grow to love you more

and more, you will feel freedom to love the things you love instead of altering what you do because you think that's what it will take to be accepted.

You. Are. Accepted. By God. And hopefully, you accept you too.

Love to read? Read.

Love to sew? Sew.

Love to make music or cakes or crafts? Make.

Remember that God created you on purpose; you are a unique recipe that does not exist anywhere else on this planet. So the things you love and the combination of your skills and desires are unlike anyone else's. And that's amazing.

When you are living out the things you love, your words follow suit. And here's a verse so you remember:

MATTHEW 12:34

For out of the overflow of the heart the mouth speaks.

I love what *The Message* says here too:

It's your heart, not the dictionary, that gives meaning to your words.

Right? Right.

I am the happiest Annie I have ever been, I think. At thirty-three, I am still single and still renting a home and still cannot curl my hair the way I wish I could. But I'm telling you, as I grow in loving me and understanding God's love for me, I am free to do the things that I really love to do—like puzzles, going to baseball games, watching *The Waltons*, writing books about things

I'm still learning, and wearing my huge slippers even when my intern makes fun of me (lay off, Connor, these are cool). You don't have to think I'm cool, because in my heart I know how God feels about me, and I am FREEEEEEEEE to be me.

(Sing it, Francesca Battistelli.)

Does that mean life is perfect? No! The tops of my white sheets are stained with mascara from crying myself to sleep a few nights ago, and I still struggle with sin and life and hurt and all the rest of it.

But in my core, things are calm. Though the storms of this life swirl around me and splash me and bruise me, my inside is calm. I am loved. I know it. And I live out of that—the writing, the speaking, the friendships, the mentor moments, all of it—starting in that deep place of knowing I am loved and learning more and more every day to love myself too.

I'm praying the same for you.

And then? Then our words can change things. Then our words, dripping with love and laced with grace, will fight against the lies and invite the Truth into every situation. And you will be known by your love.

Your Words Matter

Memorize the Word

> For out of the overflow of the heart the mouth speaks.
>
> —MATTHEW 12:34

Read the Word

- Matthew 22:30–40

- Proverbs 18:21 (Methinks you should have this memorized by now. ☺)
- 1 John 4:19
- 1 John 4:10
- Psalm 27:1–3

Journal Your Words

- Write the memory verse in your journal.
- Do you struggle with loving yourself? When did it start?
- What do you need God to say to you to help heal your heart toward yourself?
- What are some steps you can take to start loving yourself better?
- Can you list a few people (one to three) whom you could talk to about this? I know having Nichole in my life and in this conversation has helped a ton.

Use Your Words

- Do something for yourself today. Maybe buy a new bottle of nail polish (may I suggest a dark yet friendly purple?) or go on a jog while listening to your favorite album or paint something new. Just do something that reminds you that you are loved and lovely.
- Write a letter to yourself. (I know, it sounds nutso. But hear me out.) Just sit down with a piece of paper and an envelope and write yourself a note about how you WANT your life to be. What would it look like if you really loved yourself? How would your life be different if you knew how God felt about you, believed it, and lived like it? Take some time to write a letter to yourself,

like you would to a friend, encouraging her to live that way. Share verses and thoughts and encourage her (being yourself) to learn to love herself.

- Mail it. Seriously. Mail it. Put that puppy in an envelope, put a stamp on it, and ask your mom to stick it in the mail in two weeks or two days, or hand it to your best friend and ask her to mail it over the weekend.
- Read it. Believe it. LOVE YOU.

Speak Love

I'm not good at good-byes.

The night before I moved back to Nashville from Edinburgh, Scotland, the Droop family had a birthday party for their son, my good friend Harry. It was perfect—a party with all my Scottish friends but not a going-away party for me.

I don't like them. (I don't mean the Droops—I LOVE them. I don't like going-away parties for me.) When I'm the focus of such parties, it makes me too sad. I end up being a teary mess the whole time, knowing that all these people I love are at the same party because I am leaving them. Yeah, no thanks.

But at the Droops' home that night in November, it was all about Harry. And being that his personality is almost as ridiculous as my own, he loved it. There was great food, stories, and laughter like you wouldn't believe. The fire was blazing in the fireplace, as winters in Edinburgh can be so cold the chill gets in your bones.

In my memory, it is one of my favorite nights in Scotland. And in the blink of an eye, the meal was over, tea had been served, and it was time to leave.

I couldn't do it.

I looked around the room at these faces, many that I love so deeply, and realized that I was about to be an ocean away from them. While I was happy to be going home to see the people who had been an ocean away for months, I was sad to leave this new home as well.

I'm feeling that with you too. I'm not ready to say good-bye except for the fact that for you to be who God means for you to be, we have to finish.

As I'm typing, the tears are streaming and I don't want to say good-bye. I want us to sit here, and drink our tea, and pretend like we never have to leave this place.

But more than I want that, I want you to change the world, so I'm willing to say good-bye.

This week, my small group girls and I took a break from our regular Bible study and ate soup and put together a one-thousand-piece puzzle. I love puzzles, until you get to a huge section of water or sky or sand where EVERY SINGLE PIECE looks exactly the same and you have no idea how they are all going to fit together.

But with a few brains on it, we finished that puzzle. It took us four hours, but we did it.

That's what this book is, I think. A bunch of puzzle pieces that, when put together, make for a beautiful picture of a lovely girl—you—who is choosing to use her words well.

There are things we didn't discuss, to be sure. We didn't really talk about the trouble with cussing and why you shouldn't do it (but there is a whole day on it in the *Speak Love Revolution* section in the back), and we didn't spend any time on other wrong ways that you use your words—like racist jokes or screaming at a sibling or crude humor.

Think back with me to the beginning of the book. I told you this wasn't a defensive book, but an offensive one. Like a battle plan, I hope *Speak Love* travels with you and is a piece of your weaponry. I'm not here to tell you all the things you shouldn't do. I hope, instead, that you feel you are equipped for all the ways to use your words to speak love.

But if we are focused on that—if our goal, day in and day out, is to speak love with our words—those things will fall away as well. The cussing will stop because it doesn't fit into who you want to be. The sarcasm will slow because you can't imagine hurting someone else with your words, even if it is unintentional. The inappropriate jokes may still come into your mind but never out of your mouth.

You're just a different girl than you used to be.

I am too.

We have all these puzzle pieces to work with, and I hope you are starting to see the picture forming. We focus on the best things to do, and the lesser things fall away. We believe the labels that are true and trash the ones that aren't. We are intentional about the words we say to ourselves, to each other, and to God. We practice listening as well—to those we love, those we don't know, and our Father who is always speaking through the Holy Spirit and the Bible.

Also? We say thank you. I hope you say thank you a lot. Every day. Those two simple words can make the greatest impact in building up and affirming others with our words.

All the puzzle pieces. So many of them. Coming together

in just the right pattern at just the right moment to make you who God always wanted you to be and who you, maybe unconsciously, have always wanted to be.

I hope today that you will write a note. To anyone. To people who need some words of life poured over their hearts. I hope that you will stand up for people who can't stand up for themselves. And I hope you will think before you speak, choosing words that are gifts of light, not ones that cause death.

I can see you today, in my mind's eye.

I see this part of the book in your hands with only a few pages left to flip through. And I just have to wonder what else you could need from me. A hug? A hot mug of chai? A charge to go out and do the thing?

That last one, I can do. So here it is.

My friend,

I send you out of this book and into a new season of life. I commission you to go and speak love, to change the world with your words. I challenge you to never be the same person you were when you started this book. I pray you know God better, love yourself more, and see other people more clearly. I believe that you have more power of influence than you will ever know, and I encourage you to be a light that influences for Jesus.

I want to remind you of this:

Proverbs 18:21

The tongue has the power of life and death.

Yes, yes it does.

You've seen that by now, haven't you? You've seen the difference, in the stories and in Scripture and in your own life.

I send you out, my sweet friend, to speak love.

May the world never be the same because of you.

Sincerely,

Annie

Appendix

Chapter Four: Talk to God

Page 74: This is my favorite Crock-Pot recipe, and my small group girls LOVE it.

Crock-Pot Taco Soup

INGREDIENTS

- 2 pounds ground beef (you could use turkey or chicken too)
- 2 cups diced onions
- 2 (15 ½-ounce) cans pinto beans
- 1 (15 ½-ounce) can pink kidney beans
- 1 (15 ¼-ounce) can whole kernel corn, drained
- 1 (14 ½-ounce) can Mexican-style stewed tomatoes
- 1 (14 ½-ounce) can diced tomatoes
- 1 (14 ½-ounce) can tomatoes with chilies
- 2 (4 ½-ounce) cans diced green chilies

- 1 (4.6-ounce) can black olives, drained and sliced (optional)
- 1 (1 ¼-ounce) package taco seasoning mix
- 1 (1-ounce) package ranch salad dressing mix
- Corn chips
- Sour cream
- Grated cheese
- Chopped green onions
- Chopped jalapenos (fresh or pickled—whatever you like)

DIRECTIONS

Brown the ground beef and onions in a large skillet; drain the excess fat, then transfer the browned beef and onions to a large slow cooker.

Add the beans, corn, tomatoes, green chilies, black olives, taco seasoning, and ranch dressing mix, and cook in the slow cooker on low for 6 to 8 hours. (I don't like olives, so I don't include them. Sorry 'bout it.)

When I serve it to the girls, we put a few corn chips in each bowl and ladle soup over them. Then I set out sour cream, cheese, green onions, and jalapenos and let the girls add what they want on top. We never have any leftovers. Ever.

Page 79: There are lots of amazing books on prayer, but these are a few of my favorites.

- *The Power of a Praying Teen* by Stormie Omartian
- *Praying God's Word* by Beth Moore
- *Secrets of the Secret Place* by Bob Sorge
- *Passion for Jesus* by Mike Bickle
- *The Circle Maker* by Mark Batterson

Page 81: New worship albums are released all the time, but these are a few that I am going back to over and over again.

- *Worth It All* by Meredith Andrews
- *Enter the Worship Circle* (any of them!)
- *The Loft Session* by Bethel Music
- *Cutting Edge* by Delirious
- *Reason to Sing* by All Sons & Daughters

Chapter Seven: Mean Girl

Page 124: If you find yourself in a situation where you need to put out a grease fire, you are probably cooking in the kitchen. So for starters, DO NOT POUR WATER ON IT.

Instead:

- If the fire is small, cover the pan with a lid and turn off the burner.
- Throw lots of baking soda or salt on it. *Never* use flour, which can explode or make the fire worse.
- Smother the fire with a wet towel or other large wet cloth.
- Use a fire extinguisher.

Also, if you are a victim of bullies, I think this could be a good read for you: *Mean Girls* by Hayley DiMarco.

Chapter Eight: Your Online Life

Page 141: Seriously. This is the MOST DELISH french dip recipe in the world. I make it and share it all the time.

Kathleen's French Dip Sandwiches

INGREDIENTS

- 1 3-lb. boneless chuck roast
- 2 cups water
- ½ cup soy sauce
- 1 t. rosemary
- 1 t. thyme
- 1 t. garlic powder
- 8 french rolls

DIRECTIONS

Place roast in crock-pot. Add water, soy sauce, and seasonings.

Cover; cook on high 5–6 hours or until tender.

Remove meat from broth. Shred with forks and keep warm.

Strain broth and skim fat. Pour broth into bowls for dipping sandwiches. Serve meat in french rolls.

Chapter Nine: Celebrities Big and Small

Page 165: Here are some nonprofit organizations that are doing great work around the world.

- Compassion International (*compassion.com*)
- Food for the Hungry (fh.org)
- A21, an organization that helps those caught in human sex trafficking (*a21.org*)
- International Justice Mission (*ijm.org*)
- Blood:Water Mission (*bloodwatermission.com*)
- End It Movement (*enditmovement.com*)
- Help Portrait (*help-portrait.com*)

Also check out *What's Your Mark?* by Jeremy Cowart (and me!)—it is full of people doing cool things with their voices.

I love working with the Mocha Club. Join me and donate to education projects in Africa, like New Dawn High School in Kenya. (Go to *www.themochaclub.org/annie*) If you join, we'll mail you a free copy of my first book, *Perfectly Unique.* I'll even autograph it and put a scoop of glitter in the package. It's my favorite thing to do.

Page 165: I love going on mission trips. Most of the trips I've been on have been with my church, so check with your local youth group or your pastor first. But here are a few awesome mission organizations:

- Adventures In Missions (*adventures.org*)
- Youth With A Mission/YWAM (*ywam.org*)
- Young Life International (*younglife.org*)

Page 169: I'd like to thank the following musicians for playing through my earbuds at some point during the writing process:

- Sarah Jarosz
- Taylor Swift
- The Lone Bellow
- Cavetime
- Elenowen
- Imagine Dragons
- Drew Holcomb and the Neighbors
- *Downton Abbey* soundtrack
- Foster the People
- Bon Iver
- Bebo Norman
- Leagues
- All Sons & Daughters
- Justin Beiber (the acoustic album . . . duh)
- The Alternate Routes

Chapter Ten: Talking About God

Page 187: Want to read more about the Welsh Revival? Check out these resources:

- welshrevival.com
- en.wikipedia.org/wiki/1904–1905_Welsh_Revival
- *The World Aflame* by Rick Joyner

Chapter Eleven: Believe Truth

Page 204: Want to work on believing truth? Might I suggest my first book, *Perfectly Unique*? We spend a lot of time talking about that in there. Other suggestions:

- *Battlefield of the Mind* by Joyce Meyers
- *The Lies Young Women Believe* by Nancy Leigh DeMoss and Dannah Gresh

Chapter Twelve: Love You

Page 219: My friend Constance Rhodes runs Finding Balance, an incredible ministry for women that supports them as they work through eating issues and their self-image. Check out her website (*findingbalance.com*) for tons of great resources.

Also, my nutrition counselor had me read *Intuitive Eating* by Evelyn Tribole and Elyse Resch.

There are lots of online resources for healthy eating, but I would start at Constance's website. You can trust the links she shares.

Acknowledgments

I love this part of the book because I love, love, love to tell my people how I feel about them (it probably gets annoying . . . sorry I'm not sorry). And after I wrote *Perfectly Unique*, I was never sure I'd get to write one of these again. So first, let me say thanks to YOU, my sweet reader, for deciding with your hard-earned dollars that I should get to keep writing. I am grateful in deeper ways than you could ever know.

For me, books I write feel like scrapbooks of my life—no matter when you are reading this, I'm writing this today, in a particular season in my life, and this section will reflect directly, to the best of my memory, the people who stood with me as I wrote *Speak Love*.

Thanks to . . .

Girls of Grace. To the thousands of girls who show up looking for Jesus every Saturday. To Meredith Andrews, Constance Rhodes, Chris Wheeler, Amber Lehman, Point of Grace, and the amazing bands—it is my honor to share the stage with you. To the staff at Word Entertainment: Leigh Holt, Curtis Stoneberger,

Jason Jenkins, David Breen, and Josh Thompson. Thank you for believing in this message and believing in this girl. I love every single inch of Girls of Grace, and I'm so thankful to be a part.

To my Zondervan team: Jacque Alberta, you always make my books better than I could ever write. Here's to many more. Annette Bourland, you saw this book long before I did. Thanks for that. Sara Merritt, Chriscynethia Floyd, and Jonathan Michael—thank you for letting me be a crazy dreamer and partnering with me. This book is in hands because of you.

Kyle Olund—having you on my team means more than you can know. Thanks for fighting on my behalf and sifting through the mediocre to help me identify the awesome. Brian Smith and Adam Edelstein—you are keeping this ship afloat, and I will never be able to say thanks enough. Kyle Chowning, Keith Bordeaux, and Kelli Haywood—your wisdom, insight, tough questions, and time investment are incredibly valuable to me. Thank you. Corene Israel—I will never forget that you are the first person who ever published me. Every subsequent opportunity to write stems from that first yes from you. I am always grateful.

CrossPoint Church and staff, in particular Pete Wilson, Jenni Catron, and Stephen Brewster—thanks for believing in me enough to push me to be better at my craft and in my life.

My dear CP College small group—Anna Mae, Hannah C, Mariah, Jordin, Caroline, Lauren, Hannah U, April, Molly, Kendall, Sarah, Meghan, and honorary member Koula—thank you for putting up with the most insane version of me that has ever existed during the writing of this book. You were on my heart with every word that was typed. May you be the kind of women who lead others toward the cross every day of your lives.

Connor Harrell—thank you for surviving the front row seat to the beginning, middle, and end of this book, for all the glitter you scooped and all the tears you saw me shed. You are a man of integrity and humility, and I will celebrate and cheer for you all our days. Keenan Kolinsky—your faith and endurance have changed me. I am more proud of you than you can know. You two are the dearest brothers a girl could ask for and I love you to pieces. Here's to neighboring beach houses. To the rest of my Vandy boys (who will only pick up this girl book to see if they are mentioned: Look! You are!), thanks for letting me into your lives and your hearts. It is an honor every day.

Haley Watkins and Molly Scarbrough—I am grateful for the years. You understand my crazy, often better than I do. Betsy Clark—thanks for all the ways you use words to heal my heart. Lyndsay Rush and Nichole Ocepek—just a couple of rascals. Thanks for caring for me during this writing season. It was harder than I ever thought and you were there. I am indebted.

I asked a team of close friends, mentors, and family to pray for this book—from the first day to the last. To you, praying friends, I hope you see the fruits of your labor. YOU did the hard work so that I could write in peace. I'm trusting God to bless you beyond measure.

To my friends, those online and in real life, who have stood beside me and said the hard things and the loving things, and listened as I processed out loud all too much, I am grateful for you.

Daddy, Mama, Tatum, and Sally—thank you for celebrating me, supporting me, and loving me well for all these years. I am grateful that God put us in the same family.

Jesus—Your words are the ones that have forever changed me. It is only because You said, "It is finished" that I have any grace to stand on. Thank You for Your life of words well lived and documented, so that we can know how to live and speak. You saved me once, but You rescue me still, all the time. And while I am not sure of a lot of things to do with this life, I am sure of You. And I am sure of You and me. I love You with all my heart.

Contents

Introduction 247

Day 1   Your Words Matter. 250
Day 2   Poor Eve. 252
Day 3   Queen Esther 255
Day 4   Power in the Desert 258
Day 5   Gossip 261
Day 6   Twitter. 264
Day 7   Mean Girls 266
Day 8   Prayer. 269
Day 9   The Parentals 272
Day 10   Pinterest. 275
Day 11   Journaling 277
Day 12   Sounds Good to Me 280
Day 13   Brothers and Sisters. 282
Day 14   Dudes. 284
Day 15   Worship 286
Day 16   Lying 290
Day 17   Celebrities 292
Day 18   Enemies & Frenemies 295
Day 19   Cussing 298
Day 20   The Gospel. 300
Day 21   Facebook / Instagram / Tumblr 303
Day 22   Trash In, Trash Out 306
Day 23   Read On Reader 309

Day 24   Write for God. 312
Day 25   Just a Quick Note. 315
Day 26   Praying for Others 318
Day 27   What God Says About You 321
Day 28   Words Lead to Actions 324
Day 29   Memorize. 327
Day 30   Welsh Revival 329

What's Next?. 332

Dear friend,

I have an interesting invitation for you.

Want to join me in a revolution? No, we won't use guns or sing *Les Misérables* songs over a barricade, but we are going to fight.

In the past few months, I have grown to appreciate the power God has given each of us with our words. Proverbs says that words have the power of life and death, and as I look back over my life, I'm seeing how true that has always been. (I know, I know. The fact that a Bible verse is true is nothing to stop the presses over since the *whole* Bible is true, but I wanted to state it anyway.)

So I want you to join me in a word revolution. I want us to be the generation of women who focus on bringing life, not death, with our words. Call me crazy, but what if we were the generation of women who ended the mean girl mentality? What if we changed the world like that? Can you imagine it?

I can. I can see a world where people pause before they speak because what used to be okay to say is no longer okay. And I can see girls filling each other with encouragement. I can see it. And, y'all, I want to be a part of that.

I want you to be a part of it too.

So here's how this word revolution works. I've given you thirty days of short devotionals that you can read just before you head out the door or right before you fall asleep. For each day, I've included:

- The topic for that day
- A verse from the Bible
- A few thoughts from me
- A prayer you can say to God as you digest that day's devotion, expound on it in your journal, or whatever you want—it's just a guiding tool

- A revolt—an action you can take that very day to be part of the word revolution
- A space to journal and reflect on what you just read

Several days encourage you to use your words to make a difference through social media outlets. If you don't have any or all of those social media outlets, no biggie! Just do in real life what the day's revolt says to do on the computer (encourage someone, say a Scripture verse out loud, etc.).

Also, I must tell you—I don't dive fifty feet deep down into each topic. I just give some thoughts, some challenges, and some encouragement.[1] Pop over to my Facebook page (Facebook.com/anniefdowns) and let's have a discussion there!

Thanks for joining me in this revolution. I can't wait to hear how it goes for you. I'm praying for you today—that you would stand up for truth, that you would use your words to give life, and that you would see how God can use you and your words to change lives. And maybe the world.

Let's revolt, y'all!

Sincerely,

Annie

(P.S.: We're gonna memorize one short Scripture together. Hopefully, one of many for you. Keep reading . . . it's next.)

---

1   If you do want to go deeper on any of the things we discuss in these thirty days, talk to your parents, youth leaders, small group leaders, or any Christian adult you trust.

Memory Verse

PROVERBS 12:18

Reckless words pierce
like a sword,
but the tongue of the
wise brings healing.

Your Words Matter

> The tongue has the power of life and death.
>
> ### PROVERBS 18:21

The Bible can be so serious. Life and death, really? But it is true. I see that truth in my life . . . Do you see it in yours? I can tell you story after story of how someone's words gave me life and how someone's words killed something in me.

As Christian gals trying to figure out this walk with God, we need to see how revolutionary our words can be. In Genesis 1:3, God SPOKE, and there was light. We are made in His image, so we have the power to create with our words too.

For years women have struggled to use their words to give life and deny the temptation to tear others down with what they say. My prayer for you is that after thirty days, you will revolt against that temptation and change the world . . . one life-giving word at a time.

Your words matter, my friend. I can't wait to see you live it out.

Talk to God

Dear God, I'm stepping into this journey with an open mind and an open heart. I want to use my words for good. I really do. I recognize the power I have, so would You teach me how to use it? Make me more like You in these next thirty days. May the words of my mouth and the meditation of my heart be pleasing to You (Psalm 19:14).

Revolt

For today, just listen to yourself. Don't judge yourself or edit what you say. Just listen. Hear how you use your words. Listen to the conversations where you are inclined to get snippy or mad. Listen to the people whom you find it easy to love with your words, and notice the ones who make it difficult.

Wanna tell your friends that you're embarking on a word revolution? Use the hashtag #SpeakLove on Instagram, Facebook, Twitter, and Pinterest.

Journal

....
....
....
....

> Reckless words pierce like a sword, but the tongue of the wise brings healing.
>
> **PROVERBS 12:18**

Poor Eve

Now the serpent was more crafty than any of the wild animals the Lord God had made. He said to the woman, "Did God really say, 'You must not eat from any tree in the garden'?"

The woman said to the serpent, "We may eat fruit from the trees in the garden, but God did say, 'You must not eat fruit from the tree that is in the middle of the garden, and you must not touch it, or you will die.'"

"You will not surely die," the serpent said to the woman. "For God knows that when you eat of it your eyes will be opened, and you will be like God, knowing good and evil."

When the woman saw that the fruit of the tree was good for food and pleasing to the eye, and also desirable for gaining wisdom, she took some and ate it. She also gave some to her husband, who was with her, and he ate it. Then the eyes of both of them were opened, and they realized they were naked; so they sewed fig leaves together and made coverings for themselves.

GENESIS 3:1-7

Poor Eve. She was the first woman deceived by words—but not the last. God had said one thing, Satan said another . . . and Eve fell for Satan's lies. The power of words changed everything for us. EVERYTHING. Sin entered the world, shame entered our world, and Jesus paid for it with His life.

Why start this devotional on such a bummer note? Because I want you to know that your struggle to know truth from lies, and with words in general, is something you come by honestly.

It's hard to speak truth and love if your mind is full of lies. And Satan is the one who is always trying to kill, steal, and destroy (John 10:10). It's time to stop listening to the lies so you can speak the truth.

I struggled with this so much as a teenager—my mind was full of lies ("You are so ugly," "No one really loves you," etc.), so I know what that's like.

But we have to choose truth. If Eve would have chosen the true words from God, imagine how different our lives would be.

Talk to God

God, please show me any lies I believe about myself that are keeping me from speaking truth. Reveal those to me. I want to speak truth and love into the world. Help me to hear and believe Your voice over the voices that try to deceive me.

Revolt

Choose to believe God's truth today. Write the following verse on a note card and hang it on your bathroom mirror:

"But you are a chosen people, a royal priesthood, a holy nation, a people belonging to God, that you may declare the praises of him who called you out of darkness into his wonderful light." (1 Peter 2:9)

Journal

....
....
....
....
....
....
....
....
....
....
....
....
....
....
....
....
....
....

The tongue has the power of life and death, and those who love it will eat its fruit.

PROVERBS 18:21

Queen Esther

> Then Queen Esther answered, "If I have found favor with you, O king, and if it pleases your majesty, grant me my life this is my petition. And spare my people—this is my request. For I and my people have been sold for destruction and slaughter and annihilation. If we had merely been sold as male and female slaves, I would have kept quiet, because no such distress would justify disturbing the king."

ESTHER 7:3-4

It would take a ton of time to tell you the whole Esther story (but it is a good one, y'all, so you should read the whole book of Esther sometime). For our purposes, I just want to talk about her words. Here's the thing—the Bible is *full* of people who use their words well and those who don't. Queen Esther did it right—her words saved thousands of Jewish people.

She was brave with her words. Very brave. The very conversation she had with the king could have cost her life. Instead, God used her words to rescue other lives. Part of speaking life is knowing when to be brave with your words.

Want to be part of a word revolution? Be brave. Talk about Jesus to people who don't know Him. Say something nice to the girl who is always mean. Stand up for someone who's being bullied and stand by their side. Stop lies when you hear them with something as simple as, "That's not true." Ask your youth minister if y'all can go on a mission trip to a place that is outside your comfort zone. Tell your parents if a friend is cutting herself.

I promise you this—one teenage girl saying a brave thing can absolutely change the world. It could be you.

Talk to God

God, fill me with wisdom so I will know when to be brave with my words. Give me that extra ounce of courage when I need to say the brave thing. I want to do it. I want to be brave with my words. Just help me know when and how.

Revolt

Say something brave today. You can do it. I know you can. Even if it is just saying "I love you" to your family or "I am a Christian" or "Thanks for letting me sit with you at lunch." You know the brave thing you need to do. Practice today.

Journal

....

....

....

....

May the words of my mouth and the meditation of my heart be pleasing in your sight, O Lord, my Rock, and my Redeemer.

PSALM 19:14

Power in the Desert

Then Jesus was led by the Spirit into the desert to be tempted by the devil. After fasting forty days and forty nights, he was hungry. The tempter came to him and said, "If you are the Son of God, tell these stones to become bread."

Jesus answered, "It is written: 'Man does not live on bread alone, but on every word that comes from the mouth of God.'"

Then the devil took him to the holy city and had him stand on the highest point of the temple. "If you are the Son of God," he said, "throw yourself down. For it is written:

"'He will command his angels concerning you, and they will lift you up in their hands, so that you will not strike your foot against a stone.'"

Jesus answered him, "It is also written: 'Do not put the Lord your God to the test.'"

MATTHEW 4:1–7

There is so much to this story—so many topics we could talk about especially, because, you know, it's *Jesus*. But when we are thinking about using our words to create life, this story is another example of truth versus lies and how words can be life.

Jesus was faced (*like face to face*) with temptation from Satan. But Jesus stood up against the lies and spoke truth into the situation. Every time Satan offered something to Jesus, Jesus responded with a Scripture. Jesus didn't have a copy of the Bible right in front of Him—He *knew* the verses.

How cool is that? God wants us to use His words to defend against temptation. There have been times when the temptation to sin comes along and I literally can *only* stand up to it by reading Scripture out loud or singing worship songs or quoting a Bible verse I've memorized. Jesus proved that we can win against sin by using words well.

That's pretty awesome.

Talk to God

Dear God, thank You that your words stand up to lies and the temptation to sin. Fill my mind with Your words. Give me discipline to study the Bible and memorize Scripture. Thank You, Jesus, for being my example.

Revolt

Practice memorizing our theme verse, Proverbs 12:18: "Reckless words pierce like a sword, but the tongue of the wise brings healing." If you want to, post our memory verse on your

Facebook page or Twitter or make a cool graphic for Instagram or Pinterest. Use the hashtag #SpeakLove at the end of your post. Then we'll all be able to see who is memorizing the Scripture at the same time.

Journal

> May the God of hope fill you with all joy and peace as you trust in him.
>
> ROMANS 15:13

Gossip

> A gossip betrays a confidence, but a trustworthy man keeps a secret.
>
> **PROVERBS 11:13**

Somehow, in the modern-girl psyche, there is this belief that if you tell someone all the secrets you know, that makes the two of you closer friends. So instead of keeping the confidences you've promised, you just tell *one* person, because after all, she is your "best friend." Within a matter of days, the secret that only you knew is all over the school or church or Internet. And what you thought would build your "best" friendship has actually just proven that you can't keep your mouth shut.

Exposing weaknesses. Criticizing, teasing, judging in whispers. Gossip tears others down—including you. Here's how gossip tricks us: we think that when we are talking about other people that it makes us closer with the other gossipers. But the real truth? If you are talking behind someone's back with a friend, that friend probably talks behind your back too. Ouch!

I want to be different. Don't you? I mean, I feel the pull as much as you do—to whisper the thing I've heard, to share the scoop. I am not so good at doing the right thing all the time. But I'm trying. I'm wrestling with it. I'm working at it. Wanna join me?

Talk to God

Dear God, I struggle with this. I want to fit in, I want to be in the know because it makes me feel like I have a place. I want to be a good friend; I don't want to be a gossip. But sometimes I don't even realize I'm gossiping. Will you turn on the alerts in my brain? I want to be a good friend whom others can trust.

Revolt

How brave do you feel, my friend? Brave enough to stand up to gossip? I don't want to make you do something that costs you your friends (unless your friends are mean people), but if you hear gossip today, why don't you combat it by saying something nice about the victim of the gossip? Where others are trying to tear down, you toss in a sentence that will build up. Or simply walk away. In time, people will quit gossiping with you and around you. And that will be a good day.

Journal

....

....

....

....

....
....
....
....
....
....
....
....
....
....
....
....
....
....
....
....
....
....
....
....
....
....
....
....
....
....
....
....

> I have hidden your word in my heart that I might not sin against you.
>
> **PSALM 119:11**

Twitter

> My words come from an upright heart; my lips sincerely speak what I know.

JOB 33:3

Here we all are on Twitter, with a limited number of characters to say something that we hope gets attention. Whether we are trying to be funny, sexy, kind, inspirational, or downright mean, we don't have a lot of space to do it.

So you have to write smartly. Every tweet I send out from @anniefdowns takes thought and time. I know that people are reading (even if you only have one follower, someone is reading), and I know I have a chance to use my tweets to bring joy—through laughter or inspiration or whatever.

Twitter is an outlet you have to speak life, to give encouragement, to use your words to help not harm. I've heard terrible stories of teen girls using Twitter to publicly harass other girls, and it makes me sick. We aren't that kind of girls. We are the girls who use every opportunity we can find to give life with our words.

Remember this about Twitter too: once you post something, it's out there forever. The Internet has a weird way of memorizing things. So be wise with your words; be wise with your social media. Every tweet doesn't have to be about Jesus directly—mine aren't. But the goal is to be an encouraging voice in a discouraging world. Twitter is a perfect microphone for that.

Talk to God

Dear God, I want to be an encouraging voice in a discouraging world. Help me to use all my social media outlets to do that. Convict me in the moments when I'm about to use Twitter to hurt and not help. Help me to reflect You in every area of my life.

Revolt

Tweet our memory verse out to your followers (Proverbs 12:18). Use the hashtag #SpeakLove.

Journal

....

....

....

....

Give thanks to the Lord, call on his name; make known among the nations what he has done.

1 CHRONICLES 16:8

Mean Girls

> All beautiful you are, my darling; there is no flaw in you.
>
> SONG OF SONGS 4:7

We all know them. For that matter, we've already probably been one, even if just for a minute. A mean girl.

Mean girls say mean things. Mean girls use their words like bullets—they aim for your weakest spot, the place with the least armor, and shoot you. Right there.

I can still easily conjure up memories of rude and unnecessary things that other girls have said to me—about my body, my sports ability, my brain. You name it, the mean girls know how to hurt, don't they?

It reinforces what we already know—words give life or death. I wish I could tell you the magic way to make the words not hurt, or how to make a mean girl stop. But I don't have those answers. Sorry.

Here's what I will tell you: if you are the one being mean, it

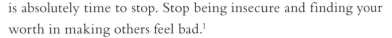

is absolutely time to stop. Stop being insecure and finding your worth in making others feel bad.[1]

If you want to combat what the mean girls say (to you or your friends), I do have that trick. Ready? *Speak words of life.* You have the same power—just use it for good! Rescue with your words where other girls have tried to kill. Be encouraging. Be uplifting. Be the voice that heals. (Think about our memory verse, Proverbs 12:18.)

And remember—the mean girls don't win in the end. Jesus wins. Every time.

Talk to God

Dear God, forgive me for the times when I used my tongue to try to hurt someone else. Change my heart. I don't want to be that girl. Give me words to encourage and lift up others. Help me to say the things that heal broken hearts and bring life.

Revolt

Put some good words out there. Post a picture of you and one of your best friends—or even more daring, someone you barely know!—on Instagram and write your favorite thing about her. Use the hashtag #SpeakLove.

---

1   My friend Manwell from Group 1 Crew says that mean girls and bullies feel bad about themselves, so they are just looking to make everyone else feel bad too. Sad, but true. If that's you, you are probably awesome; just remember that.

Journal

....
....
....
....
....
....
....
....
....
....
....
....
....
....
....
....
....
....
....
....
....
....
....
....
....

Out of the overflow of [her] heart [her] mouth speaks.

LUKE 6:45

Prayer

> This, then, is how you should pray: "Our Father in heaven, hallowed be your name, your kingdom come, your will be done on earth as it is in heaven. Give us today our daily bread. Forgive us our debts, as we also have forgiven our debtors. And lead us not into temptation, but deliver us from the evil one."
>
> MATTHEW 6:9–13

For some of you, prayer might be a brand-new thing you are just getting into. Others of you have been praying for years. To put it simply, prayer is a conversation between you and God. Jesus made it possible through His sacrificial death, so you could directly connect to a holy, perfect God.

Prayer is a two-way conversation. You can hear God in your heart, but you can also read the Bible since it is full of God's words for you.

Just as you learn and grow through conversations with your friends, the same is true of your relationship with God. The more you talk to Him, the better you get to know Him. And conversations with Him influence all other conversations.

The good news is that Jesus taught us how to pray. It isn't complicated. And you get better at it the more you practice. Like gymnastics. (I mean, I was always terrible at gymnastics, but I learned how to do a cartwheel and penny-drop into the foam pit—that counts for something, right?) Just start by praying the words Jesus modeled for us to pray. Then add in areas that are important to you—sick relatives, heartache, questions about what to do, thanking Him for all the good things in your life.

There are tons of great verses in the Bible about prayer—use BibleGateway.com to search "pray," "prayer," or "praying."

Talk to God

Dear God, I want to hear You. I want to talk to You. I want prayer to become more important to me every day. Thank You for being a living God who I can talk to. Teach me how to pray.

Revolt

Write out the Lord's Prayer (verses above) in your journal, on your blog, or on note cards to hang in your room. Just put it somewhere and read it over and over. Use this prayer as a guide to get your conversation started.

Journal

This is the confidence we have in approaching God: that if we ask anything according to his will, he hears us.

1 JOHN 5:14

The Parentals

> Honor your father and your mother, as the Lord your God
> has commanded you, so that you may live long and that
> it may go well with you in the land the Lord your God is
> giving you.

DEUTERONOMY 5:16

Let me first say, I know not everyone has a mom and dad, and that not everyone lives with their mom and dad. And some of you have parents who aren't so awesome. I know. And I'm sorry.

But let me also say this—how you speak to your parents, or the people who are performing the role of parent in your life, says less about who they are and more about what kind of person you are. We aren't here to talk about how your parents act or treat you—we are here to talk about how you should be talking to them.

The Bible makes it clear: Honor your parents. That means speaking with respect and kindness. A college student I know, Kate, does *not* get along with her stepmom. The stepmom isn't super sweet and Kate, to be honest, wasn't so sweet back. But

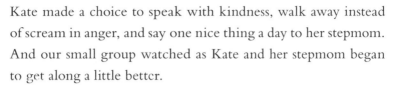

Kate made a choice to speak with kindness, walk away instead of scream in anger, and say one nice thing a day to her stepmom. And our small group watched as Kate and her stepmom began to get along a little better.

You have to remember this fact: your parents, before they were your parents, were just two humans who, like you, were hurt and healed by words. Even the best parents in the whole world make mistakes. They are often going to act like humans (meaning, not perfect). There are going to be times when their words hurt you and when your words hurt them. But remember who we are—we're the girls starting a word revolution. You can be the one to choose kindness first. Or to hold your tongue when you are angry. See what happens in your home when you watch what you say and choose to create good things with your words.

It could be pretty cool.

Talk to God

Dear God, help me to love and respect my parents. Give me the right words to show them how I feel and how grateful I am for them. Heal their broken places and help us to have a home where we speak life.

Revolt

Just tell your parents thank you today. Tell them how grateful you are for them or for something about them. You could say it in the car on the way to dinner or write it on your Facebook page (because you know your mom is seeing it there—parents love Facebook) or tweet it out to the world.

Journal

> Love is patient, love is kind. [...] It is not rude, it is not self-seeking, it is not easily angered, it keeps no record of wrongs.
>
> **1 CORINTHIANS 13:4–5**

Pinterest

> Give thanks to the Lord, call on his name; make known
> among the nations what he has done.
>
> ### 1 CHRONICLES 16:8

I am a big fan of Pinterest. You? Do you love pinning your favorite clothes and recipes and nail art? (Please, people—tell me you appreciate some crazy nail art.) The cool thing about Pinterest is that other people get to see collections of your favorite things and then share it with others.

Just like we talked about with Facebook, Pinterest is a way to use words to share truth with your friends. For a long time, I had a pin board called "Speak Love Revolution" where I pinned cool quotes I found—from the Bible, from songs, from movies—that I hoped inspired other people.

Pinterest is an easy place to influence others. Especially as we are trying to memorize Proverbs 12:18. I search for that verse to see what kind of cool art people have done with it, and then I pin it to my board. Just another way to share life-giving words.

Talk to God

Dear God, I love the way You show up in our everyday lives. I want to use everything—even my Pinterest boards—to bring You glory and fame. Thanks for the opportunity to use words to show You to the world.

Revolt

Build your own word revolution board. Then as you find awesome quotes, verses, or lyrics from your favorite Christian songs, you can pin them to the board. Use the hashtag #SpeakLove in each pin so that we can search and see them all. (Check that hashtag out—our little gal army is everywherc!)

Journal

....

....

....

....

....

....

....

....

> Do everything in love.
>
> ### 1 CORINTHIANS 16:14

DAY 11

Journaling

> Because of the Lord's great love we are not consumed, for
> his compassions never fail. They are new every morning;
> great is your faithfulness. I say to myself, "The Lord is my
> portion; therefore I will wait for him."
>
> LAMENTATIONS 3:22–24

I lead a college small group in Nashville. We spent a lot of time one year talking about the importance of journaling. It grows into a habit after a while, and there are certainly no rules to how, how much, or how often you need to journal. But once you get into journaling, it gives you a place to write down your prayers and questions and day's events and issues and praises.

Did you know the Bible is like a big journal? We can go back to it over and over to read story after story of how God was faithful to His people, how He showed up in their time of need, how He displayed His love.

And that's what your journal can do for you.

I look back on old journals all the time to remind myself of how faithful God has been in my life. I don't journal every day, but I try fairly regularly to write down the things going on in my heart. In some weird way, my own words come back, years later or days later, to encourage me in my walk with God.

You don't have to love writing to be able to journal—and you don't have to write four pages every day! Write a few words. Just a couple sentences of what God is doing. I write out my prayers too, and it's great—because it makes my brain slow down and really process what I am praying. As you journal, you will see that not only will you be able to look back and see what God has done, but you will also remember things to share with others to encourage them.

Talk to God

Dear God, thanks for Your faithfulness in my life. I am grateful for all the ways You have provided for me and cared for me. As I journal about You and our relationship, would You open up the Word to me and help me to know You better?

Revolt

We've included a journaling section at the end of each devotion to help get you going on the discipline of journaling. And whether you are starting new or are already a faithful journal writer, try to write in your journal three days in a row, recording ways that you have seen God's Word impacting each day.

Journal

....
....
....
....
....
....
....
....
....
....
....
....
....
....
....
....
....
....
....
....

Do not be anxious about anything, but in everything, by prayer and petition, with thanksgiving, present your requests to God.

PHILIPPIANS 4:6

Sounds Good to Me

> Above all else, guard your heart, for it is the wellspring of life.
>
> **PROVERBS 4:23**

I'm a huge music fan. All types. All the time. In fact, right now bluegrass music is playing through my earbuds. And I'll tell you what I love so much about music—the lyrics. I love what people are able to write—the poetry—that goes with the sounds.

That verse from Proverbs may feel like a weird left turn when we're talking about music, but here's what is true: the lyrics that flow into your ears will find their way to your heart. We need to guard our hearts, so we need to guard our ears.

I'll never be one to tell you to only listen to Christian music, but I will say you should pay close attention to the lyrics you are singing or listening to. If a song talks about self-hate or sex outside of marriage or drug use, why would you listen to those lyrics, ingest those lyrics, repeat those lyrics?

Tons of Christians are making good music—some of it is about Jesus, some isn't. I think of people like Dave Barnes, Matt

Wertz, Drew and Ellie Holcomb, Meredith Andrews, Andrew Ripp, Group 1 Crew, Lecrae, Jake Ousley, Jamie Grace, Steve Moakler, and Ben Rector, just to name a few. Those are the kinds of musicians with lyrics that matter from people who share your faith that should be on repeat in your head.

Fill your heart by filling your ears.

Talk to God

Dear God, thank You for musicians who are pursuing You and growing in their faith. I want to fill my heart with good words and good sounds. Protect me from music that will bring me down and hurt my heart.

Revolt

Share your favorite lyric or your favorite Christian artists with your friends on Facebook, Twitter, Instagram, or Pinterest. Use the hashtag #SpeakLove so we can all check out some new music.

Journal

....

....

....

> Do not conform any longer to the pattern of this world, but be transformed by the renewing of your mind.
>
> **ROMANS 12:2**

Brothers and Sisters

> If anyone says, "I love God," yet hates his brother, he is a
> liar. For anyone who does not love his brother, whom he has
> seen, cannot love God, whom he has not seen.

1 JOHN 4:20

When I was in middle school, my mom made me write this verse one hundred times. She swears she doesn't remember it. But trust me, I'm the one who sat at my desk in my bedroom, mad as a wet hen, and wrote "if if if . . . anyone anyone anyone . . . says says says . . ." for hours. I mean, *hours*.

I wasn't nice to my little sisters. I said mean things. Because of my hurts, I hurt them. And I was a Christian the whole time. So Mom decided to use words to teach me how to better use mine. So over and over I wrote this verse and began to actually understand it. *Huh! I do say I love God, and I do treat my sisters terribly—how does that work? How can that be?*

Sometimes the hardest mission field is the one in your own home, isn't it? I know, I know. Little brothers can be annoying.

Older sisters can be rude (ahem, I was). Little sisters seem to always be underfoot and big brothers are perfect. (At least, that's what I always imagined.) No matter where you fall in the sibling line of your family, you have the chance to bring this word revolution to your house.

Talk to God

Dear God, thank You for my siblings. Thanks for putting us in the same family. Even on the days when they make me crazy, I'm glad that someone else knows what it is like to grow up in our home. Help me to use my words to bring life, joy, and healing to our home. Help us to be a team who works together.

Revolt

Whether you have one brother or ten sisters, write something nice about each sibling on his or her Facebook wall or write a kind tweet about each of them. Use the hashtag #SpeakLove.

Journal

....
....
....
....

Be kind and compassionate to one another.

EPHESIANS 4:32

Dudes

Pleasant words are a honeycomb, sweet to the soul and
healing to the bones.

PROVERBS 16:24

Boys are awesome. They are. Maybe not perfect, but neither
are we, right?

How you speak to the guys in your life—from your dad
to your bros to your friends and the boys you like (and used to
like)—really matters.

My friends and I used to complain a lot about the boys here
in Nashville. I don't really know how it started, but it got to be
a habit. Frustrated, someone would say, "Uh, Nashville boys,"
and all the girls would roll their eyes.

What were we creating with our words? Nothing good,
that's for sure.

So we made a decision. About twenty of us. No more talking
about dudes like that. So we stopped. We decided instead that we
were going to build them up with our words.

You should try it. When you have the opportunity to complain about a guy—whether it is your dad or your boyfriend or your youth pastor or that guy who sits by you in class—choose instead to say something good about him. Guys have a lot of struggles (so do we, I know), but wouldn't you like to be known for the gal who cheers for the guys in her life, not the one who tears them down?

Talk to God

Dear God, thanks for making men and women. I pray for opportunities to speak life and love to the men I know. Give me the right words, with the right boundaries, to encourage the guys in my life.

Revolt

Why not encourage your dad today? Or maybe encourage one of your guy friends. Which guy in your life could use a kind word? Give it!

Journal

....

....

....

....

Therefore encourage one another and build each other up, just as in fact you are doing.

1 THESSALONIANS 5:11

Worship

> God is spirit, and his worshipers must worship in spirit and in truth.
>
> JOHN 4:24

Every time you speak, you are creating something—remember Proverbs 18:21? So when you worship, you are creating the most beautiful of things.

Worship is the best use of your words when it comes to music. Singing to God, singing about God, singing with others who believe what we believe. There is such power in worshiping with other believers—even if it is just the people on the other side of the speakers.

(Yes, worship is a lifestyle—not just what you sing—but, you know, we're starting a word revolution, so we're gonna focus on the word stuff. Cool?)

There are tons of great worship albums. Some of you may love hymns (I do) or modern worship that my grandfather says sounds like "a rock concert" (I love that too). My all-time favorite is "Cutting Edge" by Delirious?.[1] Check with your youth minister, small group leader, parents, or other Christians to see what worship albums they love.

There's this amazing thing about worship too—when we worship God, telling Him how great He is and singing about life with Him, He comes and blesses us. Seems backward, doesn't it? But that is how it works.

Talk to God

Dear God, You are so worthy to be worshiped in spirit and in truth. Help me to make worshiping with music a daily part of my life. I want my whole life to be worship to You. Use my words to worship You.

Revolt

Share a link to your favorite worship song (from YouTube or Vimeo) with your friends on Facebook, Twitter, or Pinterest. Use the hashtag #SpeakLove.

Journal

....

....

....

---

1   If you are looking for some other worship artists, check out Hillsong United, Kari Jobe, Kim Walker, Bethel Live, David Crowder, Chris Tomlin, Matt Redman, and Cory Asbury, just to name a few.

> God is spirit, and his worshipers must worship in spirit and in truth.
>
> JOHN 4:24

Halfway!

Congrats, friend! You are halfway through *Speak Love Revolution*! Is your life different? Are you loving your friends better? Journaling more? Speaking kindly to your parents?

I wonder if you are struggling. I bet you are. I am. As I am writing this, I am fighting against the temptations to use my words in all the wrong ways. It seems that when we are focused on being more like Jesus in any area, that same area has so many pressures, doesn't it?

Don't quit. We are changing things. We are using life-giving words to change our own hearts and the hearts of those around us.

Press on, sister. It will be worth it.

Lying

> But now you must rid yourselves of all such things as these: anger, rage, malice, slander, and filthy language from your lips. Do not lie to each other, since you have taken off your old self with its practices and have put on the new self, which is being renewed in knowledge in the image of its Creator.
>
> COLOSSIANS 3:8–10

I always want to tell a good story. It's in my bones. When I was younger, I would tell the best story I could think up—even if it was only partially true. When I lied about something, I always felt guilty. But I wanted to fit in, be popular, and be loved more than I wanted to be honest. Yuck.

I was growing a garden of weeds with my lying tongue. Speaking truth, telling the true story, grows beautiful flowers of life. It all goes back to the same thing, my friend—what you are creating with your words.

You have to choose the honest way, the way of highest integrity. It's more than the words you say; it is who you are. Jesus said that He is the way and the *truth* and the life. That same Jesus is the one you, as a Christian, asked to live in you. So you are already full of truth. Make sure your words reflect that.

I know it can be hard. But remember that your words are all about growing and creating something. This is your chance to change the past and become a girl who is known for her honest words.

Talk to God

Dear God, I want to radiate truth. I want the words of my mouth to flow with honesty. I want people around me to see You in the things I say. Forgive me for the times when lying was easier and I gave in to it. Strengthen me. Grow me.

Revolt

This one is easy, my friend. Just tell the truth today. Every time you get the chance.

Journal

....

....

....

> My words come from an upright heart; my lips sincerely speak what I know.

JOB 33:3

Celebrities

> The king's heart is in the hand of the Lord; he directs it like a watercourse wherever he pleases.
>
> ### PROVERBS 21:1

I think this may be my favorite day of the word revolution, and I'll tell you why: We have no idea when God is working in someone else's heart and life, and as the verse says above, God holds hearts and turns them. The loudest voices in our culture are the celebrities—what if they just need to know someone is praying for them?

A few weeks ago, I saw a segment on a late-night television show where celebrities read tweets that other people had written about them. All the tweets were mean. It was funny to watch—you know, an actress reading how someone thinks she is "overrated"—but it was also really sad. I think we forget that they are real people too. And words affect them.

What if God is already working on their heart and your tweet saying something kind draws them closer to Him?

Your words matter. Your words matter. Your words matter.

For those people in the world who hear praises like "I love you so much" from strangers and curses like "You are the worst actor ever" from strangers, we can be different.

What if God used *you* to encourage an influential voice in our culture? That's a word revolution, my friend.

Talk to God

Dear God, I pray today for the people in our culture who have so many eyes on them. Be near to them. Draw them to You. Give the Christians in Hollywood a voice to speak out their beliefs. Bless those who share their art with us. Show me who I should encourage—make it clear. And use the words I say to bring life to them.

Revolt

You probably see this one coming. Pick one or two of your favorite celebrities. Find them on Facebook or Twitter or Instagram and send an encouraging message. Share your favorite verse, pray for them, and tell them that you are praying for them. Thank them for sharing their talents with the world. Probably don't say "I love you so much" because, well, you don't really know them. Use the hashtag #SpeakLove so that we can see lots of famous people be encouraged by these gals on a word revolution. (It's gonna be fun, huh?)

Journal

....

....

....

....

....

....

....

....

....

....

....

....

....

....

....

....

....

....

....

....

....

....

....

> An anxious heart weighs a [person] down, but a kind word cheers [them] up.
>
> **PROVERBS 12:25**

Enemies & Frenemies

> "You have heard that it was said, 'Love your neighbor and hate your enemy.' But I tell you: Love your enemies and pray for those who persecute you."
>
> **MATTHEW 5:43-44**

I have some bad news for you. Someone somewhere probably doesn't like you. I know. I hate hearing it too. For my serious people-pleaser streak, this is bad, bad news.

But you know what? It's okay. Really. You are going to interact with people your whole life who think you are awesome and with people who think you are less than awesome. The truth of the matter is that how others treat you should not decide who you are or how you act. So even if you have to spend time in the same classroom as that mean girl *every day*, or deal with your brother being a punk, or hear "friends" say ugly things about you, the Bible tells us exactly what to do. Love and pray for them anyway.

Which is really easy.

Yeah, right.

I don't know that I have enemies, but I can think of two people whom I really don't care for—they each have either hurt me directly or hurt people I care dearly about. So trust me, I struggle with how to pray for people like that and how to forgive and how to love them. But I have to—I at least have to struggle through it and fight every day to be a part of the word revolution. I pray you fight that urge too—the urge to be ugly back, to tear down with words, even when it seems deserving.

Love your enemies. Jesus did. It's how the world will know that we are different—by our love (see John 13:35).

Talk to God

Dear God, it is hard, hard, hard to love people who treat me unkindly and feel like my enemies. I don't know how to do it. I really don't. Change my heart, and my words, so that I can reflect You to the world.

Revolt

Sister, hold your tongue in the moment. That's the best revolt. Silence. Don't fight back; don't gossip. I encourage you to even say one nice thing about the person who is your enemy (or frenemy). And pray. For them. For yourself. For reconciliation and forgiveness. For words of life to infuse the situation and, like a tea bag in a cup of water, change the flavor of the relationship.

Journal

> Bless those who persecute you; bless and do not curse.
>
> **ROMANS 12:14**

Cussing

> Do not let any unwholesome talk come out of your mouths,
> but only what is helpful for building others up according to
> their needs, that it may benefit those who listen.

EPHESIANS 4:29

Cussing is this thing that just falls into your vocabulary over time, isn't it? I remember hearing my friends in elementary school say words that, honestly, I didn't know. I was—and still am—an avid reader, and so it surprised me when they used words I had never heard. (I know. Such an innocent lamb.)

I wish I never felt the need to be cool and integrate any of those words—from the mildest to the perceived big ones—into my vocabulary because I wanted to be cool. But I did. And they were in the music I listened to and the movies I watched.

I know the arguments: *Who decides what words are cuss words? Why is it such a big deal? These weren't cuss words one hundred years ago . . . yada, yada, yada.* But here is the truth. If you are a part of this word revolution, and you want to speak life instead of death, cuss words don't need to be a part of your vocabulary.

They bring you down. They bring down the people around you. While we are all allowed to make mistakes, when you are trying to live a godly example in front of your friends, removing cuss words is an easy way to eliminate a stumbling block for others. You can get the same point across, no matter what you are trying to say, without using foul language. I promise, you can.

Talk to God

Dear God, please raise my sensitivity. I don't want to think cuss words or hear cuss words and not be taken aback a little. Help me to clean up my language—convict me when I'm about to speak words that aren't bringing life.

Revolt

Try this experiment. Every time you feel inclined to cuss, replace it with an audible BEEP. It won't take long until you're beeping less and are able to remove those foul words from your vocab all together. Revolt against the idea that cussing is cool. It's not.

Journal

....

....

....

> Out of the same mouth come praise and cursing. My [sisters], this should not be.
>
> **JAMES 3:10**

The Gospel

> But in your hearts set apart Christ as Lord. Always be prepared to give an answer to everyone who asks you to give the reason for the hope that you have. But do this with gentleness and respect.

1 PETER 3:15

You know what one of the absolute joys of our faith is? Telling others about it. It doesn't have to be scary; it doesn't have to be intimidating. In fact, it can mainly just be great—because you are sharing about a relationship. You are telling others about someone you love, someone who loves you, and someone who gave His life for you *and* for everyone.

I used to get so intimidated at the idea of "sharing the gospel." (Say that in a deep, manly voice, like I just did, and you'll know what I mean.) But I have learned that what draws a lot of people to deeper faith or a new faith walk with Jesus is hearing stories of how real Jesus is in my life. I don't have to have

Scriptures memorized (though I should!) and I don't have to follow some perfect script about Jesus. I just have to be prepared to give an answer for the hope that I have.

Jesus gives me lots of hope, y'all. Without Him, I would be an absolute mess. I like to say, "Jesus saved me once, but He rescues me all the time"—and it is true. So when I am hanging around with my non-Christian friends, I don't have a pamphlet on Christianity and I don't go through the Roman Road. (Google that—it's actually really cool and a great way to share about Jesus's sacrifice and resurrection.) I just like to talk about what God is doing in my life, why I chose to be a Christian in the first place, and how that relationship has shaped my life.

Don't be scared. You can't save anybody—that's Jesus's job. Just talk about Him.

Talk to God

Dear God, open my eyes to the friends around me who do not know You. Give me the right words to say. Give me the courage and the opportunity to share about what Jesus did for us all. I pray that my words will not only be life-giving but encourage someone else to make eternal life choices.

Revolt

Today, bring Jesus up in a conversation with someone who does not know Him. Then journal about the experience and pray for that friend.

Journal

> For God did not give us a spirit of timidity, but a spirit of power [...] So do not be ashamed to testify about our Lord.
>
> **2 TIMOTHY 1:7–8**

Facebook/Instagram/Tumblr

> You are the light of the world. A city on a hill cannot be hidden. Neither do people light a lamp and put it under a bowl. Instead they put it on its stand, and it gives light to everyone in the house. In the same way, let your light shine before men, that they may see your good deeds and praise your Father in heaven.
>
> MATTHEW 5:14–16

I really like Facebook. I love getting to keep up with my friends and seeing pictures of their lives. In 2011, Mark Zuckerberg (the founder of Facebook) reported that one in every nine people on Earth has a Facebook account. If your friend group is anything like mine, it's more like eight out of nine (including my mom).

You know what is cool about Facebook, and other social media like Instagram and Tumblr? They give us an outlet, every day, to say whatever we want to the people who are our friends. It's exactly what girls like us want—a way to share life-giving words. A way to start this word revolution. I have a friend in Scotland who, almost every day, says something on Facebook about what God is doing in her life. It's not every post, and it's not annoying; it's just her real experience. I like that. It encourages me.

One of my favorite things about Instagram is creating word art of verses or quotes and posting them. I also like taking a picture with my friends and posting it, so that my friends know how grateful I am for them! As in all cases, Instagram can be a mean and ugly place, but we are there to bring light! So we post things that encourage others, not intentionally make them feel left out. We use our artistic sides to create posts on Tumblr or Instagram that are life-giving.

(P. S.: You know what is REALLY fun? When we get to use something that wasn't meant to make God more famous—like Facebook or Tumblr or Instagram— and use it to bring Him fame. That's pretty rad.)

Talk to God

Dear God, thank You for my friends. Thanks for connections and the opportunity to use social media to bring You glory. Help me to see how I can use my time on each of these outlets to encourage others and help people see You. I am Yours, my whole life—including my Facebook page, Instagram feed, and Tumblr.

Revolt

Encourage your friends to join this word revolution. Here's a status update that you can post: Hey, girls! Join me in the Speak Love revolution—30 days to change our world! #SpeakLove

Journal

Each of us should please his neighbor for his good, to build him up.

ROMANS 15:2

Trash In, Trash Out

> The good man brings good things out of the good stored up in his heart, and the evil man brings evil things out of the evil stored up in his heart. For out of the overflow of his heart his mouth speaks.
>
> LUKE 6:45

When I was in college, I listened to a variety of music. Most of the songs I enjoyed were fine, but a few (truthfully, a few of my favorites) had more than one cuss word in them. I thought it was no big deal to listen to them once in a while . . . or once in a week . . . or once in a day.

One night, my roommates and I sat down to dinner in our apartment. I honestly don't even remember what we were talking about, but all of a sudden, when I went to say something, I said the f-word. The big one. They stopped talking and eating and stared at me. Then they turned pale, and their eyes bugged out. But so did mine. I had never intended to say that; it just came out. The moment that word shot out of my mouth, I knew exactly which song had put it in my head. I jumped out of my chair, ran to my room, and deleted that music immediately. Seriously, I did. Then I returned to the table and continued to eat dinner, totally embarrassed.

You know what went wrong here? I had allowed all sorts of rubbish in and that is what came out. I'm not going to give you rules on what kind of things you should listen to, read, or watch. I'm simply going to tell you this truth: what you let into your mind fills your heart. What fills your heart comes out of your mouth. Just pay attention; you'll see that you are more inclined to cuss when you hear it and more likely to be disrespectful when that is what you see in movies. It's weird but true.

Again, no rules here. I just want to encourage you to guard your heart and mind so that the words that come out of your mouth are like a river of crystal clear water. No trash.

Talk to God

Dear God, I want to glorify You by guarding what I let in. Open my eyes to entertainment that is uplifting and edifying. Raise my sensitivity to things that lead to words of death.

Revolt

For the next seven days (the rest of this devotional), go on a trash fast. Take a break from TV and movies, step away from ungodly music. Focus on books about God and your relationship with Him. Listen to music that glorifies God. After seven days of this trash fast, you'll be surprised at how you don't miss it, how foul language shocks you, and realize how much better life is when you are filling your mind with good things.

Journal

Create in me a pure heart, O God, and renew a steadfast spirit within me.

PSALM 51:10

Read On, Reader

> All Scripture is God-breathed and is useful for teaching, rebuking, correcting and training in righteousness, so that the man of God may be thoroughly equipped for every good work.
>
> **2 TIMOTHY 3:16–17**

I am a pure book nerd. From childhood when I used to read in the bathtub (and drop books in the water all the time) to now as an adult when I usually would rather read than do almost anything else, books have been my constant companion.

I became a Christian when I was five, so the Bible has always been a part of my reading life. But I haven't always enjoyed it. To be honest, parts of it are just plain boring—lists, laws, and things that my brain doesn't quite understand. As I have matured in my faith, I have grown to see the Bible for what it really is—not some boring old book that Christians have to read, but a collection of stories, lessons, and love from

God to us. I love reading it. In fact, I have a reading plan where I try to read the Bible in a year. I'm on my second round, and it's going fine so far.

Lots of great Christian books are out there—authors who love God and are working hard to write things that are interesting and entertaining and meaningful for you in your walk with Christ. I think of people like Emily Freeman, Ann Voskamp, Tricia Goyer, Sandra Byrd, Shannon Primicerio, Mary DeMuth, Catherine Marshall, Elizabeth Elliot—women who have used or are using their gifts to give us books to read, both fiction and nonfiction, that teach us about Jesus.

These are the exact kinds of things we should be putting into our minds to make sure that the words that flow from our hearts to our mouths are life-giving.

Talk to God

Dear God, thank You for Your Word and how the Bible is living and active and is real in our world today. Increase my love for the Bible, my desire to read it, and give me a heart that loves to study Your Word.

Revolt

What is your favorite book by a Christian author? Share that title and author on your Facebook page or on mine (Facebook.com/anniefdowns)! Make sure to use the hashtag #SpeakLove so we can all check out the new, awesome books out there.

Journal

> The heart of the discerning acquires knowledge; the ears of the wise seek it out.
>
> **PROVERBS 18:15**

Write for God

> They overcame him by the blood of the Lamb and by the word of their testimony; they did not love their lives so much as to shrink from death.
>
> ### REVELATION 12:11

The "him" mentioned above is the same "him" from Day 2—that nasty serpent, the devil. I love this verse because it reminds us that we are already victorious—we have everything we need to defeat the enemy in our lives.

You were saved by the blood of the Lamb (Jesus), and the word of your testimony overcomes the enemy and his temptations. That's why I do what I do, y'all. I spend my life writing out stories of God's faithfulness, daily testimonies, so that the enemy doesn't win in my life and so others can be encouraged by the way God moves in me.

God does the same for you, you know. He is always working on your behalf. Sometimes you just have to look around to see it. You may not be a natural-born writer—that's fine. You may not enjoy writing at all—that's cool. (We can still be friends.) But at certain times in your life, doors may open for you to write about God. Take those chances! We overcome the enemy by the words of our testimony.

If you love to write, my friend, write on. Write every day. Whether it is a status update, a blog, or a book, pour your heart into words and then share some of them with the world.

Think of all the books you've read after which you could say, "Wow, that book changed my life." It was the power of words. The power of someone else sharing their testimony. And now it is your turn. Share, share, share. Write of His love, write of His faithfulness. We all have stories to tell—every single one of us. Tell yours. For the glory of God.

Talk to God

Dear God, use my words to bring You glory. Whether they are in my journal, in notes to others, online, in a school newspaper, or on a bookstore shelf, use my words to draw people closer to You.

Revolt

Whether you love to write or not, you should write down your testimony—the story of when and why you decided to accept Jesus to be your Lord and Savior. You don't have to have a crazy testimony (I don't) to have a story that God can use to draw people to Himself. You never know when you are going to get the chance to share that, and it is powerful!

Journal

....
....
....
....
....
....
....
....
....
....
....
....
....
....
....
....
....
....
....
....
....
....

Let your light shine before [others], that they may see your good deeds and praise your Father in heaven.

MATTHEW 5:16

Just a Quick Note

> A word aptly spoken is like apples of gold in settings of silver.
>
> **PROVERBS 25:11**

Don't you love snail mail? As much as email and texting is certainly faster and easier, there is something beautiful about a handwritten note.

Before my small group girls went home for the summer, we each wrote our addresses on five envelopes. Then we traded envelopes, and everyone left with five letters to write and mail. Throughout the summer, I would go to my P.O. Box with my fingers crossed that there would be a note from one of the girls in there.

There is something really powerful about kind words written down for a friend. As the verse says, when you use your words well, they are priceless to those who receive them.

You can save notes like that, the ones that people mail you for encouragement. In fact, throughout my journals over the years, I have taped notes that have spoken to my heart.

It doesn't take a lot of time, but a handwritten note is a gift that can impact someone forever. Don't take this day lightly—a few minutes prayerfully hovering over a note that you mail to a friend could bless her and change her life in ways you don't know. Words create life, remember?

This is your moment, sister. Write a note. Share life. Give encouragement. Mail the gift of words to people who may need it more than you could ever imagine.

Talk to God

Dear God, bring to mind all the right people who need an encouraging note today. Lead me to the right verses to share and the best words that will bring life. May these notes that go out honor You and bring You glory.

Revolt

Stop by the store and get a stack of cards from the stationery section. Buy some stamps, ask some of your friends for their home addresses, grab your favorite pen, and send out some notes. Share your favorite Bible verse or one that means a lot to you right now. Encourage your friends by talking about the favorite qualities you see in them. Then put a stamp on it and mail that puppy.

(You know, call me crazy, but you could mail notes to your family—yes, the ones who live in your house—if you wanted to. Or your small group, Young Life, or youth leader. Adults need encouragement too!)

So send out five notes, snail-mail style, to people you care about.

Journal

....

....

....

....

....

....

....

....

....

....

....

....

....

....

....

....

....

....

....

....

....

....

....

....

....

Let us consider how we may spur one another on toward love and good deeds.

HEBREWS 10:24

Praying for Others

> I thank my God every time I remember you. In all my prayers for all of you, I always pray with joy because of your partnership in the gospel from the first day until now, being confident of this, that he who began a good work in you will carry it on to completion until the day of Christ Jesus.

PHILIPPIANS 1:3–6

I think I don't know how powerful prayer really is. I mean, I pray for my friends and I have definitely seen God move in their lives, but sometimes I forget that prayer is a tool God has given us to directly affect the world.

I hope you pray for your friends. I hope you pray for your family. But I know firsthand that sometimes it's hard to remember all the people we need to pray for. My friend Katie taught me a cool trick a few years ago: I have seven note cards, each with a different topic written on it (family, friends, future, my church, the world, etc.), and on them I keep a running list of important prayer requests or needs. I also put stars beside my prayers that God has answered. With these cards, I flip through them daily and pray for a few minutes over each of them.

Praying for others takes the focus off of you. If you just pray for yourself and your own needs all day every day, that will lead to a pretty selfish lifestyle. It does good things for your insides to take words of prayer and turn them toward other people.

Pray for your people. Take them before God, and ask Him to move on their behalf.

Talk to God

Dear God, I am grateful for the people You have placed in my life. Give me a heart that loves to pray—especially for others. Open my eyes to the prayer needs of those around me. Teach me how to pray for my friends and family members.

Revolt

Make a list of five people at the end of this devotion that you can commit to pray for, using the lines below. It can be family or friends or whomever you want—just pick five and pray for them every day this week. Ask God to bless them, and pray for their needs (you could even ask them if they have anything they want you to pray about). If they don't know Jesus, pray for their salvation.[1] The Bible says to watch and pray—do it and watch God move.

---

1 You could also make note cards like I've done—it has helped my prayer life SO much!

Five people I can pray for:

....

....

....

....

....

Journal

....

....

....

....

....

....

....

....

....

....

....

....

....

....

....

> Dear friend, I pray that you may enjoy good health and that all may go well with you.
>
> 3 JOHN 2

What God Says About You

> But you are a chosen people, a royal priesthood, a holy nation, a people belonging to God, that you may declare the praises of him who called you out of darkness into his wonderful light.
>
> ### 1 PETER 2:9

Here's another truth for your truth basket. (I don't know what makes me think you have a truth basket, but let's just go with it.) The reason we are able to use words to encourage and speak life into others is because God is always encouraging us and speaking life into us—if we are listening.

This is a beautiful reason to spend time reading and studying the Bible. It is full of verses meant to affirm who *you* are. Throughout the Scriptures, God has written out words about each of us—like the verse above—that you can cling to.

When I need to be reminded that God loves me, there is

verse after verse, like Psalm 100:5, to tell me that. When I need to be reminded that God has a plan for my life, I just have to flip to Jeremiah 29:11.

When I forget that I am forgiven, I go back and read Psalm 103:11–12 and am reminded of how God has removed my sin as far as the east is from the west (that's far, y'all).

You see, He knows the power of words because He created the world with them. When God speaks words of life over us, it changes who we are. And then, in turn, we get to pour words of life over our friends, family, *and* people who don't know Jesus.

Read what God says about you. Digest His words. Believe them. Enjoy them. And know that they are for you.

Talk to God

Dear God, thank You for filling the Bible with verses about who I am in Christ. I want Your love for me to be my whole identity. Do that in me. Open the Bible to me so I can see the verses that tell of Your love for me.

Revolt

Post Jeremiah 29:11 on Instagram, your Facebook page, Twitter, or add it to your Speak Love Pinterest board. Hashtag it #SpeakLove.

Journal

....

....

....

"For I know the plans I have for you," declares the Lord, "plans to prosper you and not to harm you, plans to give you hope and a future."

JEREMIAH 29:11

Words Lead to Actions

> Dear children, let us not love with words or tongue but with actions and in truth.
>
> 1 JOHN 3:18

I used to teach elementary school, and each year for the first few days all I did was teach the classroom rules to all the students.[1] We would practice walking in line, how to go through the cafeteria to get lunch, and how the overall rules worked.

My words would instruct them and they would act in response to that. That is the definition of obedience.

You already know by now that your words have power and can create life or death. The other thing your words can do? Cause action. What you say can lead others to act.

I mean, take this whole devotional, for example. Here I am, sitting in a hotel room in Charlotte, North Carolina, writing

---

1   You remember those first days of each new school year from your childhood, don't you?

about the power of words. And there you are, wherever you are, responding to those words.

Words lead to actions.

If you tell yourself over and over how ugly you are, your actions will reflect that. If you keep speaking life over your little sister, she will act in confidence. That's why it is important to use your words well; they are going to lead to action, in your own life or in someone else's.

Your words, my friend, are so powerful. Please, don't forget that.

Talk to God

Dear God, as I seek to live and use my words to glorify You, help me to remember the power of what I say. When I speak to others, and when I talk about myself, I want those words to lead to actions that further Your kingdom.

Revolt

Ask one or two friends to buy or download *Speak Love*, then meet together to take action. Pray for each other, mail cards to some of their friends or family, brainstorm how you each can share words of encouragement at home, etc. Get ready to act.

Journal

....

....

....

The good [person] brings good things out of the good stored up in [their] heart.

LUKE 6:45

Memorize

> Your word is a lamp to my feet and a light for my path.
>
> ## PSALM 119:105

We are twenty-nine days in! I am so hoping that you already have Proverbs 12:18 memorized. If not, you better get to practicing, sister!

The first verses I remember memorizing came thanks to some kids' music. The tapes (yes, cassette tapes—google it if I lost you) were called GT & the Halo Express, and each song taught me a different verse. I lost those tapes years and years ago, but last year for Christmas (as an adult, by the way) I got the entire CD set of those songs. And I still listen to and still love them, thank you very much.

Here's the thing about memorizing Scripture—no matter where you are, if you know verses by heart they will encourage and uplift you. For the things you struggle with the most, memorize Scripture to fight off those temptations. The verses that speak to you of God's love and His heart for you—if you have those locked away in your brain, you always know them.

How do you decide what to memorize? Start with verses that you love. You could also choose verses your pastor or your youth minister uses. Pull up BibleGateway.com to find verses that are topical, like if you want to memorize Scripture about God's love. Or you could go back and memorize some of the verses in this devotional.

Hide His Word in your heart. It will change everything.

Talk to God

Dear God, I want to hide Your Word in my heart. It isn't easy memorizing Scripture, but I want to do it. Please open my mind to be capable to latch onto these words. Lead me to the Scriptures that are on Your heart for me to memorize.

Revolt

Write out our memory verse (Proverbs 12:18) *without* looking. Post it on Facebook, Twitter, Instagram, or Pinterest. Use the hashtag #SpeakLove and then you'll be able to see all the other gals around the world who are memorizing the same Scriptures as you.

Journal

....

....

....

> I have hidden your word in my heart.
>
> **PSALM 119:11**

Welsh Revival

> Though you have not seen him, you love him; and even though you do not see him now, you believe in him and are filled with an inexpressible and glorious joy, for you are receiving the goal of your faith, the salvation of your souls.

1 PETER 1:8-9

You wanna hear about a serious word revolution? You want to hear how one teenage girl changed everything with one sentence?

Then read about the start of the Welsh Revival in 1904:

In February 1904, the Spirit of God bade [Pastor Jenkins] introduce some new feature into the young people's meeting held after the morning service, and it dawned on him to ask for testimony, *definite testimony*, as to what the Lord had done for their own souls.

One or two rose to speak, but it was not testimony. It was just then that the same young girl [named Florrie Evans, who had been afraid to give her life to Christ the night before]—shy, nervous, intelligent—stood up in tears and with clasped hands simply said with a deep pathos, "Oh I love Jesus Christ with all my heart." Instantly, the Spirit of God appears to have fallen upon the gathering . . . It was the beginning of the visible manifestation of the Spirit breaking out in life.

Several reports say that this confession was what set the church on fire for God. Can you dig that? One teen girl. *One sentence* about Jesus. And it sparked a revival in the whole country.

Those are some powerful words.

I chose this to be our last day together on purpose. Because from the day I heard this story, it has not stopped rocking my world. The idea that a teenage girl being brave enough to say that one sentence—"I love the Lord Jesus with all my heart"—could change an entire country has me absolutely fired up.

That could be you.

Those words gave life and life to the full, didn't they?

So as we part ways, I hope you read 1 Peter 1:8–9 again. I hope you memorize it. I hope that you live it every day.

Even though you have not seen Jesus, you love Him.

And even though you don't see Him now, you believe and are filled with joy.

Tell somebody.

Your words matter. Use them.

Talk to God

Dear God, at the end of this word revolution, I just want You to know that I don't want to be the same anymore—I don't want to be the girl who started this thirty days ago. I want to be a revolutionary. I want to change the world with my words. Open doors. Show me how. Let me reflect You with my words.

Revolt

Post Florrie's proclamation, if it is true for you, on Facebook, Twitter, Instagram, or whatever social networks you use. Use the hashtag #SpeakLove.

Journal

I can do everything through him who gives me strength.

PHILIPPIANS 4:13

What's Next?

What now? That's a great question, and I think you are the best one to answer it.

How is your life different? How has this thirty-day word revolution changed the way you write, speak, type, and even think? What has God done in your heart?

Journal about it if you haven't been journaling all along. Write about the result of the time you poured into this study.

Dear friend, well done. We have revolted together and changed something in the world. And it is going to keep getting bigger.

Want to keep going with the word revolution? Get a bunch of your friends to buy or download this book, and go through it again—this time you lead the group. Keep checking into the #SpeakLove hashtag and comment on what other girls around the world are saying about changing the way we Christian women use words.

This has been so fun, y'all. So, so fun. I hope it is just the beginning of some amazing things God is going to do in our lives.

Thanks for walking with me through this. I'd love to hear about your experience. Will you pop over to my Facebook page (Facebook.com/anniefdowns) and let me know? I want to hear what God is doing in your life!

Just remember—your words matter. Every day.

To God be the glory!

Sincerely,

Annie

Perfectly Unique

Love Yourself Completely, Just As You Are

Annie F. Downs

In *Perfectly Unique*, bestselling author and sought-after speaker Annie F. Downs shares her humor and her wisdom to help pre-teen and young adult women understand how, from head to foot, the way you view your body is directly connected to how you serve God.

From the thoughts you think to the steps you take, every part of you is part of your spiritual journey.

Your body is a sacred treasure, a worshipful instrument, a unique masterpiece! But sometimes it feels confusing, awkward, or flawed. The truth is you and your body, all of it, are important and beautiful, designed especially by God with a specific plan and purpose! That's a pretty big deal.

Whether you are looking for new ways to love God more fully and understand his love and purpose for you or trying to figure out why God made you as you are, *Perfectly Unique* will take you on a thoughtful, funny, and spirit-filled exploration of the way you were designed and will help you better honor the creator by learning to value his perfectly unique creation—you!

Available in stores and online!

100 Days to Brave

Devotions for Unlocking Your Most Courageous Self

Annie F. Downs

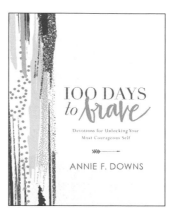

You were always meant to be brave.

Whether you're making a major decision, dealing with a difficult transition, or facing a fear, *100 Days to Brave* will give you courage and confidence to move forward.

Annie F. Downs felt her challenges were too difficult, too scary, too much. Then she decided to stop allowing fear to hold her back. It wasn't easy or simple. But it was good.

With honesty and relatable humor, this compilation of best-of writings and new pieces from Annie will give you the inspiration to embrace the path and the plan God has for you and experience personal growth.

Dare to spend the next 100 days discovering that you are braver than you know and stronger than you thought possible.

Available in stores and online!

About the Author

Annie F. Downs is a best-selling author, nationally known speaker, and podcast host based in Nashville, Tennessee. Her books include *Perfectly Unique*, *Remember God*, *100 Days to Brave*, *Looking for Lovely*, and *Let's All Be Brave*. Annie hosts the popular weekly *That Sounds Fun Podcast* and is a huge fan of bands with banjos, glitter, her community of friends, boiled peanuts, and soccer. Read more at anniefdowns.com and follow her on Instagram @anniefdowns.